Ancient Peoples and Places

CENTRAL AND SOUTHERN ITALY

General Editor

DR. GLYN DANIEL

ABOUT THE AUTHOR

David Trump was educated at the King Edward VI Grammar School, Chelms-ford, and Pembroke College, Cambridge, where he graduated in Archaeology and Anthropology in 1954. After a season with Dr. Kenyon at Jericho he began research on the Apennine Bronze Age in Italy, with the help of the Rome Scholarship in Classical Studies. After another foray to the east, Baluchistan, he held a Research Fellowship at Pembroke College, during which he received his doctorate. From 1958 to 1963, he was Curator of Archaeology at the National Museum of Malta, carrying out fruitful excavations on several sites there and at Ariano in Italy. He is now a Staff Tutor with the Board of Extra-Mural Studies at Cambridge.

Ancient Peoples and Places

CENTRAL AND SOUTHERN ITALY
BEFORE ROME

David Trump

81 PHOTOGRAPHS
50 LINE DRAWINGS
10 MAPS
I TABLE

FREDERICK A. PRAEGER
Publishers
New York · Washington

THIS IS VOLUME FORTY/SEVEN IN THE SERIES
Ancient Peoples and Places
GENERAL EDITOR: DR. GLYN DANIEL

BOOKS THAT MATTER

*Published in the United States of America
in 1965 by Frederick A. Praeger, Inc.,
Publishers 111, Fourth Avenue
New York 3, N.Y.*
© *David Trump 1966
Library of Congress Catalog Card Number: 65–20081
Printed in Holland*

CONTENTS

ILLUSTRATIONS

6

7

9

Preface

PREHISTORIC STUDIES in Italy have not proceeded uni-
formly. As elsewhere in Europe a sporadic interest in antiquities can be detected at a very early date. For example Giovane
was comparing the Bronze Age settlement in the Pulo di Molfetta with primitive villages in America and Australia as early
as the beginning of the eighteenth century. But in a country so
wealthy in the remains of Greek, Etruscan and Roman civilisations, it is not surprising that the humbler relics of the more
distant past attracted little attention. When they began to do so,
from the middle of the nineteenth century onwards, it was
largely for their real or imagined importance as ancestors to the
classical civilisations. This period of research reached its climax
in the last decades of that century and the first of this. Such
names as Chierici, Brizio, Colini, Ridola, Quagliati, Orsi,
Taramelli and above all Luigi Pigorini spring to mind. If the
theories tended occasionally to outstrip the discovered facts, the
novelty and enthusiasm of the research can be held largely to
blame. In 1909 T. E. Peet published *The Stone and Bronze Ages
in Italy*, summarising admirably the work to date.

Some measure of the decline in interest which followed is
given by the fact that his book has never been adequately replaced, in English or Italian. Patroni's *La Preistoria* in 1935 cannot claim to come near it, being overweighted with destructive
criticism. For this period between the wars, Ugo Rellini is
probably the only archaeologist to rank beside the giants who
had gone before. The works of synthesis now, though useful,
were all more narrowly specialised, MacIver on the Iron Age,
Rellini on the Apennine Culture, Säflund's re-assessment of
the *terremare*, and so on.

13

Since the Second World War, interest has reawakened to an extraordinary extent, and enormous strides have been made in both the quantity and quality of the excavations. The work of L. Bernabò Brea at Arene Candide and Lipari was the first and most outstanding, but many other workers have followed in the area more strictly covered by this book, the peninsula. Of these it would be invidious to single out individual names, or even particular bodies from among the university institutes and *Soprintendenze alle Antichità* by which the greater part of this research has been organised.

In many ways therefore this is an opportune moment for a general work on the prehistory of Italy. Interest is greater than ever before, there is a vast amount of newly disclosed material, much of it unfamiliar to archaeologists outside the country, and this material has drastically modified many long-held ideas. On the other hand it is for the same reasons an extraordinarily difficult moment to attempt the task. Peet was writing when that first wave of activity had broken and was expending itself on the beach. There is nothing to suggest that the present wave is spent or even at its crest. Far from it.

This means that new material is coming to light at a great rate, or is already in existence but not yet made available by publication. Naturally any theories and generalisations here offered can take into consideration only what is already accessible to scholars. Even there, in a work of this length there is rarely space to consider adequately all the alternative explanations yet put forward, so an author has often to choose which he considers the most satisfactory one, and deal sketchily or not at all with the others. I apologise in advance for the occasions on which I must seem more authoritative and dogmatic than the evidence really justifies. Of one thing I am convinced – that this book will be superseded after a much shorter currency than Peet's.

During the ten years in which I have been interested in the prehistory of Italy, I have had help from many people. To everyone of them this book owes something; without them it would not have been possible for me to write it.

In particular I would mention Pembroke College, Cam/ bridge, the British School at Rome and its ever/helpful staff under Mr J.B. Ward Perkins, the National Museum of Malta under Capt. C. G. Zammit, the Apulia Research Committee of the Society of Antiquaries of London and its chairman the late Professor Sir Ian Richmond, and the publishers of the series, Thames and Hudson, and its General Editor, Dr Glyn Daniel, who made different phases of my research possible.

In Italy I have had assistance, stimulation and encouragement from too many to be able to thank them all by name. Some cannot be allowed to pass without mention, I hope without giving offence to the others – Professors G. Annibaldi, L. Ber/ nabò Brea, L. Cardini, A. DeFranciscis, N. De Grassi, P. Gra/ ziosi, G. Lo Porto, M. Pallottino, R. Peroni, S. M. Puglisi, A. M. Radmilli, P. C. Sestieri and Stazio; Drs G. B. Buchner, D. Lollini, C. E. Østenberg and S. Tinè; and the late Professors A. C. Blanc, C. Drago and A. Maiuri. Where I have disagreed with any of these, it is always with regret and apology. Acknow/ ledgment for the photographs is made more explicitly on p. 190.

Special mention is due to the friends, English and Italian, who helped in the excavation of La Starza. Nor can I pass without reference the loss suffered by prehistoric studies in Italy when John Bradford became unable to complete his valuable work on the Tavoliere. How much this book and its readers owe to my wife is known only to her and myself.

Finally to be acknowledged is the debt all archaeological writers should recognise, to the unnumbered and unnamed potters, metal/workers and flint/knappers without whose hum/ ble products they would have nothing to study.

D.T.

CHRONOLOGICAL TABLE

Note that the dates are approximate and that the scale is logarithmic, i.e. the space devoted to the earlier periods is proportionally much less than is that for the later ones.

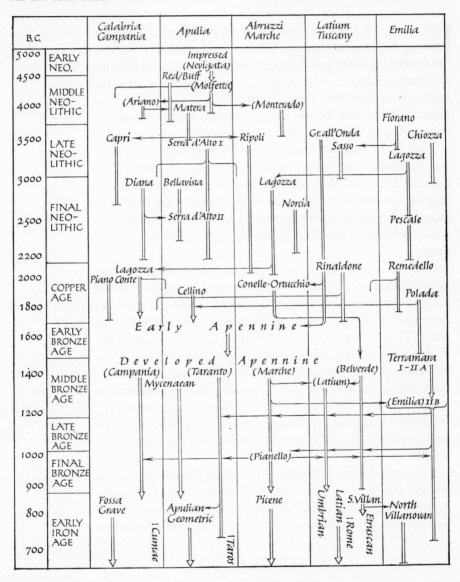

CHAPTER I

The Country

ITALY SHOWS MANY CONTRASTS in its scenery and this
variety is clearly mirrored in its history and prehistory. Indeed,
the further back one goes into the past, the less control over his
environment does man have, and so the more control does that
environment have over him. Until cultural unity followed the
political unity won by the Roman armies, Italy was not one
country but at least four, often many more.

Two of the most obvious of these, the large islands of Sicily
and Sardinia, have already been described in this series by L.
Bernabò Brea and Margaret Guido respectively. The fact that
their stories are so different shows the effects of the territories'
geographical isolation. Only slightly less obvious are the two
units which go to make up mainland Italy, the north and the
south.

Curving in a wide arc from the Riviera to Yugoslavia is the
Alpine chain, with the French, Swiss and Austrian frontiers
keeping closely to its crest. Below this and within the curve lies
the sweep of the Po valley, a wide and practically featureless
plain. Though topographically so different, the two are linked
by fingers of valley reaching back into the mountains, spurs of
hill country projecting into the plain, and spectacular lakes
lying astride the dividing line. Culturally, too, it is difficult to
separate the two areas. Together they form Continental Italy,
Alt' Italia, which looks across the passes to the Rhône, Rhine
and Danube valleys of Central Europe rather than south across
the Mediterranean.

In contrast is the peninsula, still extraordinarily varied but
welded into a unit by the 600 mile range of the Apennines
running its whole length and by the Mediterranean which
washes its two long sides and southern end. In width it nowhere

17

exceeds 130 miles. Amid or bordering the mountains are areas of plain but all are comparatively small, too small to have form⁄ed independent entities for any length of time. The greater part of its area however is neither mountain nor plain but hill country, fertile and varied.

Since its history, with few and minor exceptions, followed a completely different course from that of the north, it has been thought better to separate the two regions, to allow each to be dealt with adequately in a volume of its own in this series.

It is often difficult to keep in mind the slope of the Italian peninsula. The 'South' could be described no less accurately *Fig. 1* as 'East'. For example, Rome is further east than Venice, al⁄though on the opposite, western, coast. At the same time it is on the latitude of the Gargano. The range of the Apennine Mountains which forms the spine of the peninsula does not even maintain a uniform south⁄easterly direction but follows a markedly sinuous course. By cutting obliquely from coast to coast at its northern end, it forms a natural frontier across the neck of the peninsula. On the Tyrrhenian side it runs so close to the sea that passage is easier across the low passes behind Genoa than it is along the narrow and often interrupted western coastal belt northwards from Pisa and the Arno valley. Liguria tends therefore to follow the fortunes of the Po valley to its north rather than those of the peninsula to its east. Here a convenient limit for this book is the boundary between the regions of Ligu⁄ *Fig. 2* ria and Tuscany, roughly along the line of the River Magra near La Spezia.

On the Adriatic side it is harder to draw a line since the watershed here swings southwards to leave a corridor of low hilly country some 30 miles wide giving easy communications far down into the peninsula. The regional frontier between Emilia and the Marche, just south of Rimini, suggests itself. Republican Rome chose the Rubicon, just north of that town. For the earlier periods of prehistory either would serve equally

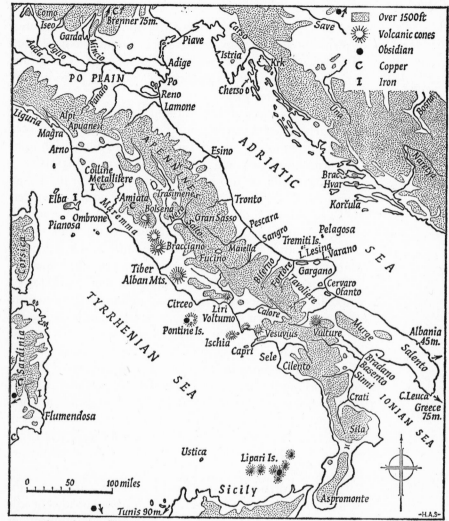

Fig. 1. *Physical map of Italy*

satisfactorily, but in the Bronze Age peninsular peoples advanced beyond this line as far as the River Reno. This takes in
the eastern half of Emilia, known as the Romagna, and the city

19

of Bologna. Under the Etruscans further advances into the Po valley to the north and west were made, but these lie beyond the scope of this book.

Settlement in this area was concentrated on the narrow belt of open country between the Apennine foothills, here often a difficult clay terrain, and the swampy open plain. It is the same line that the Via Emilia later followed, and for the same rea-sons. The prehistoric sites cluster thickly around Bologna itself, and to a lesser extent at Imola and Faenza. These three towns lie close to the Reno, Santerno and Lamone valleys, all giving access to Apennine passes into Tuscany.

Fig. 59

At Rimini this open zone fuses with the narrow coastal plain but from this point the hill country, with a more stable subsoil, becomes the more desirable. Consequently the ancient sites are found along the alternating valleys and hill ridges inland rather than on the coast itself. They cluster particularly thickly along the Sentino, south-west of Ancona. This must in part be ex-plained by the more thorough research here, but again is surely affected by the nearness to the passes of the Scheggia and Vico, giving comparatively easy passage into Umbria. The former, rising to a little under 2,000 feet, is the lowest in Central Italy.

Plate 10

Plate 13
Fig. 45

The pattern of hill and valley continues south unaltered through the Marche, the Abruzzi and the Molise as far as the River Fortore on the borders of Apulia. In front of it the smooth Adriatic coastline is another unifying factor, until interrupted by the promontory of the Gargano. Behind it, however, the Apennine chain breaks up into more or less isolated blocks of limestone mountain, Monte Vettore, the Gran Sasso d'Italia (at 9,584 feet the highest in the peninsula) and the Maiella. Even here the Apennines nowhere form an impassable barrier.

On the western side there is a greater variety of scenery. First come the Alpi Apuane, a fantastically rugged range of hard limestones and marbles, the latter extensively quarried at Car-rara. Then comes the famous countryside of Tuscany, a series

Fig. 2. *The regions and provinces of the peninsula. Towns
containing museums with important prehistoric collections are
marked with ringed dots. Note direction of the compass point*

of small plains enclosed by vine-clothed hills and threaded like beads along the River Arno. The more important ones lie around Arezzo, Florence, Lucca (more accurately on the River Serchio) and Pisa. South again, the hills of Chianti rise gradually past Siena to the Colline Metallifere and Monte Amiata. Though of no very great height these are, as their name suggests, of exceptional importance for their metal ores, copper and iron in particular. Off the coast are rocky islands like Elba, again rich in iron, and Monte Argentario, though the latter is now attached to the mainland by sand spits.

Inland lies Umbria, a continuation of the Arno country into the basin of the upper Tiber. The Val di Chiana has at different times been drained into each. Again there are small plains, at Sansepolcro, Foligno-Perugia, and on Tiber tributaries at Terni and Rieti. Between these rise more limestone hills, now largely terraced for vineyards.

Latium shows even more variety. A swampy coastal plain extends from the Tiber's mouth through the Pontine Marshes. Another new element of scenery is introduced by a series of extinct volcanic craters, most of them containing lakes like Bolsena and Albano. Associated with these are extensive tracts of tuff, a compacted volcanic dust giving a characteristic level countryside cut by sudden gorges. North-east, east and south-east are alternating valleys and limestone ridges, the outermost, Monte Circeo, once an island. Inland they run back into the wild mountain country of the inner Abruzzi. Here was another large lake, Fucino, drained in 1870. Like Trasimene near Perugia but unlike the lakes of Latium it is not volcanic in origin, being a large solution-hollow in the limestone with its underground outlets blocked by impermeable clays.

Campania is somewhat similar. It, too, has coastal plains at the mouths of the Garigliano (or Liri), Volturno and Sele rivers. The volcanic zone is represented by the extinct cone of Roccamonfina and the still or recently active Vesuvius, the

Plate 5

Fig. 29

22

Phlegraean Fields and Ischia, with which the Pontine Islands   *Fig. 52*
should be included. Tuff from Vesuvius floors the Terra di
Lavoro, the extremely fertile and densely populated plain be׳
tween its foot and the first limestone mountains of the Apen׳
nines above Caserta and Salerno. Inland there are again open
valleys, the Volturno and Calore, and bare uplands. The latter
are lower than behind Latium and leave a wide corridor of
clay country across the watershed into northern Apulia. Here
one can again cross Italy's mountainous back׳bone keeping
below 2,000 feet. As a route going back to prehistoric times
this corridor, named after Ariano Irpino at its centre, will call
for mention many times.   Plate 4
     The valley of the Cervaro beyond the watershed leads into a
district unlike any described yet, the Tavoliere. This is the larg׳   Plate 1
est plain south of the Po valley. Low hills, fringing the Apen׳
nines and the rivers that flow from them, break down into a
near׳featureless plain between Foggia and the sea. Half of its
coastline is blocked by the limestone massif of the Gargano, the
spur of Italy, projecting into the Adriatic. This is an isolated   Plate 14
but archaeologically very interesting corner of the country.
     Beyond the River Ofanto, Apulia changes completely. The
bare limestone hills of the Murge are separated from the Adriatic
by a belt of country now densely planted with olives and al׳   Plates 2, 7
mond trees. South׳east again, the Salentine peninsula, the heel
of Italy, extends past Lecce as far as the cliffs of Cape Santa
Maria di Leuca. This is a continuation of the bare rock of the   Plates 6, 8, 9
Murge at a much lower altitude. Inside the heel lies Taranto,
its fine natural harbour making it an obvious centre of com׳
merce from a very early date.   *Fig. 39*
     Lucania, alternatively known as the Basilicata, has contrasts
too, but less crisply marked. In the far north, overshadowing
Melfi, is the extinct volcano of Monte Vulture. In the east
around Matera are limestone hills very like the neighbouring   Plate 3
Murge. To the west the mountains rise higher again, where the   *Fig. 9*

watershed has swung back to the Tyrrhenian side of the penin/sula. Beyond the interruption of the inland Diano plain they continue into the hill country of the Cilento in southern Cam/pania as far as the west coast. The centre is taken up by a poor country afflicted by soil erosion and, until recently, malaria. Its seasonal rivers, the Bradano, Basento, Agri and Sinni, finally cut through the coastal dunes to the Ionian Sea.

Apart from small coastal plains, around the lower Crati river for example, Calabria is a land of mountains. There are three distinct groups, the Apennine chain, here hugging the west coast, the solid block of the Sila, and another chain build/ing up to the peak of Aspromonte in the extreme toe. From here one looks across Reggio di Calabria and the Straits of Messina to Sicily. Though separated by a low corridor west of Catanzaro, the last two groups are of the same ancient meta/morphic rocks, but there are no minerals here to compare with those of Tuscany and Sardinia.

Finally a word must be said on the routes of access to the peninsula. Most obvious are those from Northern Italy and beyond, by the Ligurian coast from the south of France (little used), the Adriatic coast from Yugoslavia and the Alpine passes from Central Europe. From Emilia these would continue south across the Apennines into Tuscany or along the coast into the Marche.

Three sea routes connect the opposite shores of the Adriatic. Navigators from Dalmatia would make a landfall between Ancona, the only natural harbour on that coast, and the Gar/gano, where Pelagosa and the Tremiti Islands provide convenient stepping stones. From Epirus and Albania, by the short sea/crossing, they would reach the heel of the peninsula. From the Gulf of Patras or the Aegean they would pass the Ionian Islands to land on the inside of the heel or elsewhere on the Ionian coast. They would soon have discovered the Straits of Messina, beyond which Sicily and the Tyrrhenian would lie open before them.

Finally, routes connect with the west through Sardinia, northabout by Elba and Corsica or southabout by Lipari and Sicily, and so on to Provence or the Balearics and Spain. By these, the new ideas reaching Italy from the east were passed on to start off similar developments in the west.

The peninsula was clearly very well-favoured for prehistoric settlement. It has kindly soils and climate, and natural resources of flint and copper. Further, it is somewhat withdrawn from the turmoil of the continent, yet open to the sea lanes of the Mediterranean. Its development frequently benefited from the arrival of foreign traders or refugees, and was rarely interrupted by invasion.

CHAPTER II

The Palaeolithic and Mesolithic

A S IN MANY other parts of the world, the climatic changes
associated with the advance and retreat of the ice through
the Pleistocene period have left their mark in Italy. In the north
are clear signs of the Alpine glaciers in the shape of lake-filled
glaciated valleys and systems of moraines. In the Apennines
the traces of ice action are fewer, mainly ice-formed cirques in
the higher peaks. More widespread are the signs of changing
sea-levels due to the waters being locked up in the ice in colder
periods and released to swell the oceans in the warmer ones.
This was a world-wide phenomenon but the names for the
different stages recognised, Sicilian, Milazzian, Tyrrhenian and
Monastirian, are taken from the coasts of the Riviera and Sicily
where they were first studied.

We should perhaps begin the story of man in Italy with the
bones of *Oreopithecus*, the ape discovered in the Pliocene lignite
mines of Gavorrano in Tuscany. Although not human, and
only distantly related to our human ancestors, he does show the
possibility of exciting future discoveries in this field. Certainly
our knowledge of the earliest periods of Italian prehistory have
broadened remarkably as a result of researches in the last few
years.

The first sure signs of man's presence in the peninsula date
to the end of the second interglacial around 200,000 years ago.
Sporadic Abbevillian and Acheulian hand-axes of flint from
this period of warmer conditions have been found practically
everywhere in the country. Recently they have come to light
in great numbers on two major sites, the Valle Giumentina
near Chieti and at Venosa near Melfi (Matera province), where
they lay in gravel deposits washed into lakes by the swollen
rivers of the third interglacial. They enable us to form some

Fig. 3

Fig. 3. Acheulian hand-axe from the Chienti valley, Macerata

picture of the way of life of the primitive hunters of the time, using their all-purpose hand-axes to grub up edible roots or dismember the carcases of beasts trapped on the way to their drinking places.

Even more vivid is the picture given by a third site, Torrim-pietra just west of Rome. Here the late Professor A.C.Blanc discovered an actual camp of Lower Palaeolithic man. Beside the hearths and traces of windbreaks or light huts were hand-axes, flakes and bones tossed aside after the meal was over. After the site was abandoned it was buried and preserved by many feet of volcanic ash thrown out by violent eruptions of the craters of Bracciano and the Alban Mountains. What is more difficult is to imagine the people themselves, since barely half a dozen fossilised fragments of their bones have been found in the whole of Europe, and none at all in the Italian peninsula.

At Torrimpietra and elsewhere, the axes chipped from flint cores were accompanied by lighter tools shaped from flakes – the Clactonian and, later, the Levalloisian industries. In the course of the last interglacial these developed into industries of

27

the Mousterian type forming the Middle Palaeolithic. Several versions are known widespread through Italy but so far in no very great quantity. It cannot be long before they are discovered in undisturbed rich deposits; then study will be able to reveal more accurately their relationships. Of particular interest are the first 'Italians' known, Neanderthal skulls from Saccopastore at the gates of Rome and from caves on Monte Circeo 60 miles to the south-east. These are the 'cave-men' of popular imagination, with beetling brows, retreating chin and stooping gait.

In the latter part of the last glaciation men more like ourselves made their appearance. Their tool kit, finer and more varied than anything known earlier, typifies the period of the Upper Palaeolithic. Though tools of Aurignacian type, as found in France and Central Europe, are not common in Italy, the later Gravettian appeared in both quantity and variety. For the first time we see clear local variations, named after Montebello di Bertona, Pescara (the Bertonian), and the Grotta Romanelli beyond Lecce (the Romanellian). The earliest radiocarbon date, 10,670 ± 410 BC (all carbon dates, be it noted, are approximate, their accuracy decreasing as one goes further back into the past), came from the Grotta Ortucchio in the Fucino basin. It was associated with Bertonian material and a human skull of Cro-Magnon type, an early form of modern man.

Fig. 29

Art of this period has been found in recent years. Though later in time and less imposing than the great cave art of France and Spain, it is still valuable evidence for human advance in the world of ideas. Notable are engravings of animals on the cave walls of Romanelli and Romito (Papasidero near Cosenza) and paintings have been reported from the Grotta Paglicci in the Gargano. Engravings on bones and pebbles are more widely known. All hint at hunting magic, by which in primitive belief man can increase his success in the chase. Other and obscurer ideas are implied by the Palaeolithic 'Venus', a corpulent figurine carved in stone, found near Lake Trasimene in Umbria.

Fig. 4

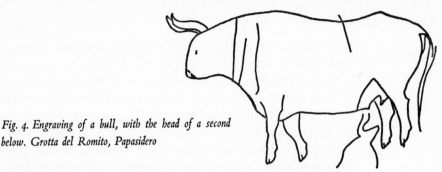

Fig. 4. Engraving of a bull, with the head of a second below. Grotta del Romito, Papasidero

The tendency to produce smaller flint tools continued as the climate improved after the last retreat of the ice. The Mesolithic industries of Italy need a good deal more study before even their outlines can be firmly drawn; this they are now receiving. Derived from the Upper Palaeolithic, they continue down to the arrival of the Neolithic food-producers around 5000 BC.

Through the whole of this immensely long period, man was a hunter and food-gatherer, depending solely on such things as his skills could garner of what nature provided. In cold periods there were wild goats, chamoix and deer. When the ice had gone, the first two disappeared and the third became scarce. There remained smaller prey like birds and fish, and of course roots, berries and nuts were much more frequent. But such supplies are scanty and unreliable and could have supported a population of no more than a few thousands, perhaps only a few hundreds, in the whole of the Italian peninsula.

There is therefore a good economic reason for the incredibly slow development of human culture at this time. With food so scarce, all man's energies had to be applied to one endeavour – the struggle for survival. In good times he over-ate, in bad times he starved. Putting aside for the future was next to impossible and leisure for thinking of ways to improve his lot non-existent. The nomadic life prevented him from gathering together any but the simplest and most portable of material possessions. In short, his life was barely distinguishable from that of the other animals which shared the country with him.

29

CHAPTER III

The Neolithic

EARLY NEOLITHIC

Fig. 5

SOMEWHERE ABOUT 5000 BC the first Neolithic farmers to reach Italy arrived by sea from the other side of the Adriatic. Finding the rocky shores of the Gargano little to their liking, they pushed on along the coast to a more promising district, a broad estuary where the rivers of the Tavoliere reached the sea near the modern town of Manfredonia. Here they set up their camp beside the inlet on a low hill now known as Coppa Nevigata.

Many things marked off these people from their predecessors in Italy, their boats for a start. If the Palaeolithic and Mesolithic hunters were unable to cross to Corsica, Sardinia or Malta – no remains of theirs have come to light on those islands – they certainly could not have made the journey from Dalmatia. The huts the newcomers set about building themselves had stone wall footings and beaten earth floors, far more sturdily constructed than the temporary shelters of the wandering hunters. One of the first tasks of the women was to find a local supply of clay to model into domestic pottery, a material too heavy and fragile for use in nomadic hunting camps. The men's stone axes had their flaking edges ground smooth, a small but important detail which modern experiments have shown increases their efficiency to a surprising extent.

Fig. 5. Palaeolithic and Neolithic sites. Only the more important are indicated. Other figures referred to give detailed maps or views

1. *Torrimpietra*
2. *Saccopastore*
3. *Monte Circeo*

4. *Fucino (Grotta La Punta, etc.)*
   See Fig. 29
5. *Montebello di Bertona, Penne*

6. *Valle Giumentina, Chieti*
7. *Grotta Paglicci, Rignano, Gargano*
8. *Venosa*
9. *Grotta Romanelli*
10. *Grotta del Romito, Papasidero*
11. *Grotta della Madonna, Praia a Mare*
12. *Fiorano Modenese*
13. *Alpi Apuana (Grotta all'Onda, etc.)*
14. *Riparo della Romita, Asciano, and Grotta del Leone, Agnano, Pisa*
15. *Grotta dell'Orso, Sarteano*
16. *Grotta Lattaia, Monte Cetona*
17. *Ripabianca di Monterado*
18. *Grotta Frasassi, Gola del Sentino. See Fig. 45*
19. *Santa Maria in Selva*
20. *Norcia*
21. *Luni*
22. *Sasso di Furbara*
23. *Petescia, Valle Ottara, Cittaducale*
24. *Ripoli di Corropoli, Vibrata valley*
25. *Villaggio Leopardi, Penne*
26. *Grotta dei Piccioni, Bolognano*
27. *Grotta delle Felci, Capri*
28. *La Starza, Ariano Irpino*
29. *San Domenico, Tremiti Islands*
30. *Grotta Scaloria, Manfredonia*
31. *Coppa Nevigata*
32. *Tavoliere, Foggia (Passo di Corvo, La Quercia, etc.)*
33. *Pulo di Molfetta*
34. *Grotta le Mura, Monopoli*
35. *Grotta Ostuni*
36. *Taranto (Scoglio del Tonno, Bellavista, Leporano, etc.) See Fig. 39*
37. *Matera (Setteponti, Serra d'Alto, Murgia Timone, La Murgecchia, Tirlecchia, Grotta dei Pipistrelli, etc.) See Fig. 9*
38. *Grotta Sant'Angelo, Cassano*
39. *Girifalco*
40. *Lipari (Diana, Castello, etc.)*

But by far the most important items in the cargoes being unloaded were a few jars or leather bags of seed-corn, wheat, barley and lentils, and some sheep and calves trussed to prevent their upsetting the balance of the boats on the voyage. For the newcomers had learnt the techniques of farming, by which man can produce food near his home instead of having to pursue it wherever it could be found. By modern standards the methods of husbandry were primitive, the return pitifully small and the dangers of crop failure or loss of stock through disease or wild animals appalling. Despite this, the new skills represented an enormous step forward which paved the way for all future advance in human culture. Above all, a comparatively assured, settled and storable food supply gave man for the first time leisure to think, to plan for the future.

The discoveries which lay behind this change had been made perhaps two thousand years earlier in the Near East and knowledge of them had then spread slowly as more farming land was needed for the growing population. The routes by which it reached Italy are still far from clear. The impressed decoration of Italy's earliest pottery is similar to that found in the Starčevo Culture of Yugoslavia, which must provide its immediate origin. A curious motif, the so-called rocker-pattern described below, hints at even more distant connections, with Tell Mersin in southern Turkey, much nearer the original sources of the farming economy. But it is only a hint, as the design appears at other periods elsewhere in the world, the Sudan, Mexico and Manchuria for example, where direct links are unlikely.

Plate 15

The new methods of food production did not completely sweep away those of food collection, however, any more than they did elsewhere. Even today, wild rabbits, winkles and blackberries are still appreciated as food. At Coppa Nevigata the staple diet seems to have been the cockles which abounded in the estuary. In the 7 feet of rubbish which accumulated during the life of the village, shells were the commonest find,

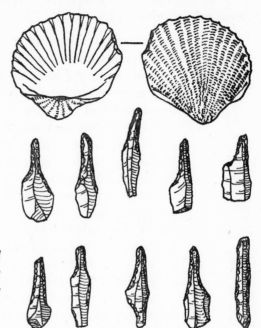

Fig. 6. Awls of the Sipontian industry used for opening cockle shells. The opened shells are shown above. Coppa Nevigata. (After Puglisi)

Fig. 6

each with its edge damaged near the hinge. In the same deposits were found the small flint awls responsible for this, the equiv⁄alents of our modern tin⁄openers. Apart from some simple knife⁄blades and scrapers these are the only tools to have sur⁄vived.

The flint cockle⁄openers seem to have been specially devel⁄oped for this purpose because they have not been found on other sites, where more reliance must have been placed on crops and stock for food. All sites have produced bones of domestic animals and at Prato Don Michele on the Tremiti Islands, north of the Gargano, was found a blade showing the charac⁄teristic gloss flint acquires when it is used in a sickle for cutting corn. Southwards from Coppa Nevigata, villages and caves occupied in this period are known as far as Polignano beyond Bari, all significantly close to the coast. The settlers of Nevigata

33

were not the only ones to venture across the Adriatic to open up the newly discovered land.

What links these sites is their distinctive pottery. Common, variable, fragile, yet in fragments almost indestructible, this is the most useful of man's handicrafts from the archaeologist's point of view. Here the characteristic feature is a decoration of
Plate 15
impressions produced on the surface of the soft clay before the pot was baked, by jabbing it with the ends of sticks or the wavy edges of shells, or by prodding or pinching it with the potter's finger-tips. The object seems to have been solely to roughen the whole surface, the flat bases and the necks of some jars being the only parts spared. No attempt at design was made either by an orderly arrangement of the impressions or by reserving a smooth background. Two other methods were used rather less frequently: rocking a shell-edge to and fro across the wet clay to leave a curved zigzag printed on it, and irregularly slashing the surface with a sharp point of wood, bone or flint. This is clearly a version of the great family of Impressed Wares found at the very beginning of the Neolithic sequence throughout the Central and West Mediterranean.

The vessel shapes have no more claim to elegance than has
cf. Plate 16
the decoration. Bowls, curved buckets and globular jars with cylindrical necks, the Italian *bottiglia,* are the only forms, all heavily decorated and all with coarse out-turned bases. Some jars were given clumsy handles. The bowls were usually burnished inside by polishing with a pebble or bone slip before the firing. This has the effect of compacting the surface and making it more watertight as well as improving its appearance. Otherwise the fabric of the pot is always thick and porous, with a pale grey or buff-coloured surface. It was serviceable, but even allowing for the fact that on its arrival there was no other to compare it with, this pottery can hardly be claimed as beautiful. Even its makers seem to have felt the same about it because it survived in this form for only a short period.

MIDDLE NEOLITHIC

The Middle Neolithic is marked by two changes in the pottery. Firstly, an element of design appears in the Impressed Ware. *Fig. 7* The impressions tend to be applied in rows rather than falling haphazardly and some areas are even left without any, particularly at the rim and near the base. This is still clearer on the incised vessels, which now have simple geometric patterns of hatching instead of the earlier indiscriminate slashing.

Secondly, a new and much finer pottery was introduced for the best dinner services, the Impressed Ware pots being relegated to the kitchen. That some such distinction was made at the time is shown by the fact that the Impressed Ware is never found with repair holes – when it broke it was thrown away. But the new Red on Buff Painted Ware was too fine to be lightly discarded. If it met with an accident, holes were drilled on either side of the break so that the pieces could be bound together again. This in turn suggests a concern for material possessions, one of our earliest glimpses of a proud and thrifty housewife: irked by the breakage, she attempts to make good the damage until the family can afford a replacement.

This ware was worth taking trouble over. It is beautifully made of compact clay, thin and smoothly polished, its colour orange-buff to creamy white. The surface may be left without decoration or carry a simple bold design painted in broad bands of scarlet. These may be straight L's or zigzags, or curved arcs or running swags. At one site in Calabria, Sant'Angelo di Cassano, two oval or lozenge-shaped blotches of paint, one on either side of the pot, were the only decoration. On some sites in northern Apulia white paint, alone or together with red, was occasionally employed but the sherds of this type so far found are too small to give a clear idea of the designs produced in this way. *Plate 20* *Plates 21,22*

The vessel shapes are also much more artistic and again we have evidence that the potter was aware of this. A number of bowls have a thin line of red paint on their very lip as their only

Plates 20, 21

Fig. 12
Plate 22

ornament, hardly a decoration in itself but serving admirably to focus attention upon the vessel's form. This is always smoothly curved, an open, hemispheric or globular bowl with a round base. Sometimes a straight insloping neck is added to make the shape known to the Italians as a *vaso a tocco*. No handles are ever found on these though a few heavier jars with handles and flat bases are known.

In the later or Molfetta form, the Impressed Ware, nearly always accompanied by that painted in Red on Buff, is found over the whole of south-eastern Italy. The Early Neolithic colonisation in the Gulf of Manfredonia had obviously prospered and spread rapidly from its centre on the Tavoliere. The appearance of the painted ware may imply reinforcements of new immigrants from beyond the Adriatic, since its original home must lie in that direction. Unfortunately we cannot fix its source more closely until the opposite shore of the Adriatic has been more thoroughly explored.

Plate 1, Fig. 10

A second painted ware occurring at some of the Tavoliere villages, particularly La Quercia, we can relate specifically to Greece. It shows the same curious effect as can be seen on the Sesklo Ware there, a blurred edge to all the painted lines as if the potter had been too impatient to let the paint dry properly before carrying out the burnishing. This painting is in narrower lines forming hatched bands or triangles. It is often found on the same vessels as a rocker-patterned decoration derived from the local Impressed Ware, an interesting fusion of two traditions. Either technique can occasionally be used to produce more ambitious designs, such as stylised human figures. A few jars were given crude and frightening human faces to protect their contents from harm.

Fig. 7

Plate 2

The type site for the later variety of Impressed Ware is the Pulo di Molfetta, 15 miles west of Bari. This is an extraordinary circular cave of which the roof has collapsed, leaving an open hole in the rock 400 feet across with vertical 100 foot walls. On

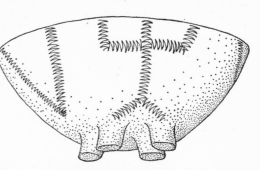

Fig. 7. Footed bowl with a human figure worked in rocker pattern. From the Bradford excavation at the Masseria Villana, Lucera

its floor were found traces of a village of simple oval huts with clay floors and stone footings for walls. Fragments of clay daub preserved by accidental baking show the clear imprint of the wattle framework of the upper walls on which it had been smeared; the roof would presumably have been of thatch. A hearth in one corner provided warmth and cooking facilities. Why this inaccessible spot should have been chosen for the settlement remains a mystery.

Beneath the olive groves now surrounding the Pulo was found the resting place of its Neolithic inhabitants, a cemetery of over fifty burials. These enable us to add the human figures to any reconstruction of the scene. They were of typical Mediterranean stock, short, slight, long-headed and almost certainly dark, and would attract no notice in Southern Italy today. Each skeleton lay flexed or crouched in its trench grave, to imitate the foetal position or the posture of sleep, or simply to take up less space. A ring of stones sometimes surrounded the body. Within it lay a few personal ornaments, tools and pots for the dead person's use in the other world or on the journey towards it.

This was not the only type of hut in use at the time. On a village site at Penne in the Abruzzi traces of a group of huts survived in the form of oval hollows in the ground averaging 10 feet across and 3 feet deep. The wattle-and-daub walls here would have risen from the ground surface without intermediate footings. Added importance was given to the site by the discovery of charcoal which, when subjected to radiocarbon analysis, yielded a date of 4630 ± 135 BC. The pottery showed the same mixture of Molfetta Impressed and Red on Buff Painted Wares as we have noticed in Apulia at this time.

Even deeper below ground were the dwellings in the natural caves which occur freely in the Italian limestones. It is easy to dismiss a cave-dwelling as primitive and squalid, as indeed it can be. But many are commodious, dry and draught-free, far warmer in winter and cooler in summer than any open-air hut. Their possibilities as homes were realised from a very early date and some, within the city of Matera for example, are still lived in today.

Plate 3

Fig. 8. The stratigraphy in the Grotta della Madonna, Praia a Mare. Bottom was not yet reached. (After Cardini, in the Pigorini Museum, Rome)

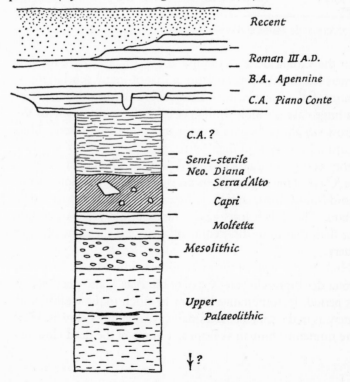

Recent

Roman III A.D.

B.A. Apennine

C.A. Piano Conte

C.A.?

Semi-sterile
Neo. Diana
    Serra d'Alto

Capri

Molfetta

Mesolithic

Upper
    Palaeolithic

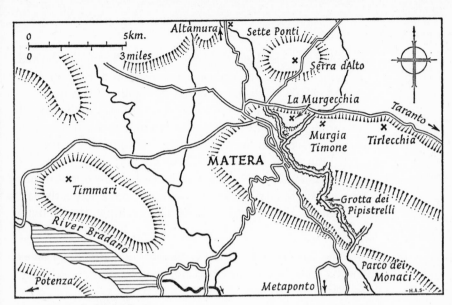

Fig. 9. Sites in the Matera district

In the Grotta della Madonna above Praia a Mare the first farmers left their rubbish on top of that of many generations of hunting folk. Later-comers also recognised the advantages of this huge cave set high in the coastal cliffs with a view of the narrow Calabrian beach for many miles north and south. They in turn added layers of their refuse, recording unwittingly their history as if in the pages of a book. At the Grotta dei Piccioni (the 'Cave of the Pigeons'), in the side of a gorge at Bolognano, inland from Chieti, certain of these layers were dated by radiocarbon. The earliest level gave a figure of 4295 ± 130, a little later than that from the Penne village, with the same types of pottery.

High in the wall of the great gorge below Matera opens the Grotta dei Pipistrelli (the 'Cave of the Bats'), also occupied at this period. Its importance lies not so much in the wealth of its pottery as in the contents of a small cave opening below it. Here were numerous human skeletons, a home of the dead close be-

Fig. 8

Fig. 9, Plate 3

Plates 15, 18, 21, 22, 23

side that of the living. The Grotta della Scaloria, with a magʹ nificent view of the Tavoliere, was also extremely rich in pottery. This site is less easy to interpret, since it is far too narrow and tortuous to live in and too remote to have served as a rubbish tip. Nor did it yield any more evidence than other sites of having served a religious function, the likeliest alternative explanation. In fact these people have left us nothing from which to infer their religion, beyond the hints of belief in an afterʹlife offered by their burial rites.

The most remarkable settlements of this period are undoubʹ tedly those of the Tavoliere, the plain around Foggia in northʹ ern Apulia. The R.A.F. flew many photographic sorties over this region in 1943 to study enemy airfields and traffic moveʹ ments on the east coast railway. In working over these for their military information, John Bradford noticed certain unexplainʹ ed dark circular cropʹmarks where the vegetation had parched

cf. Plate 1
Fig. 10

less quickly in the Italian summer. In 1945 he was able to study some of these settlements on the ground and to continue reconʹ naissance from the air for more. Some features he could date to the medieval period, more to the Roman and a great number to the Middle Neolithic. There were thus three distinct and superimposed landscape patterns, in the right circumstances still visible to an eye trained to look for them.

The individual huts had been built on the surface of the rock and so had left only scanty traces in the form of clay daub. They had however been grouped into compounds, as in a modern African *kraal*, each compound surrounded by a roughly circuʹ lar ditch perhaps 70 feet in diameter with a wide entrance. It was the depth of soil in these ditches which held the moisture to cause the cropʹmarks seen in the photographs. Sometimes traces of stone walls survive along their inner lips. On small sites a single compound would have attached to it a yard or

Plate 1
Fig. 10

bailey, similarly ditched, making a small homestead. On larger sites a number of compounds, from two to a hundred or so,

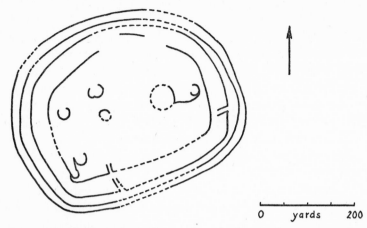

Fig. 10. Plan of village on the Tavoliere 4 miles south of Foggia; four concentric ditches with inturned entrances enclosing hut-compounds. (After an air photograph by J. Bradford)

would be gathered to form a village or even a town. This would in turn have a ditch or ditches around it, again often with a bailey or home-field alongside.

The village at La Quercia had no less than eight such concentric ditches. The site at Passo di Corvo, 6 miles north of Foggia, must surely from its size be considered a town. Its 10 foot-deep triple ditches enclosed an area 500 yards by 800, containing a hundred compounds. This was the largest and latest of three successive settlements on the site, succeeding two homestead compounds, and from the evidence of its pottery belongs to the latter part of the Middle Neolithic.

Although these sites are virtually invisible from ground level before excavation, their ditches having been deliberately refilled when no longer needed, they must rank with Europe's most remarkable prehistoric field antiquities. A single site is impressive; how much more so the nearly three hundred recorded from the Tavoliere, an area the size of Kent. A comparison of the population this implied with the figure suggested for the Mesolithic period gives some measure of the results of the new farming economy. A whole bustling world can be conjured up from the dark rings which appear in the cornfields for a few weeks every summer.

These ditches seem at first glance obviously defensive. A single circuit would be ample to prevent the most nimble cow or even goat from straying. Additional features such as in-turned entrances and stone walls along the inner lips of the ditches again look like village defences. Yet in the great wealth of material recovered from sites of this date no weapons have been recorded beyond a few sling-bolts. Even arrowheads do not occur until the Final Neolithic. Perhaps further work in this fascinating area will suggest some other explanation for the ditches, or reveal that warfare broke out in Italy at an earlier date than we had believed.

The material from the villages and caves enables us to fill in many details of the way of life of their inhabitants. Flints with *Fig. 36* sickle gloss and stone querns for grinding the corn are quite frequently found. Both probably represent the women's share of the family work, the fields and their crops. Cultivating the fields tends to become man's work only with the introduction of the plough at a later date, since the domestic animals needed to pull it are usually his responsibility. Cattle, sheep, goat and, to a lesser extent, pig are all commonly represented in the rubbish of these settlements. An early excavation report mentioned buf-falo bones but these have not been found again. Deer antlers from some sites show that a little hunting was still carried on, even more surely a male task. Whether the dogs whose bones are sometimes found were employed for guarding the stock or for hunting one cannot tell.

The tools for these and other purposes were of the simplest types. There is nothing looking like a hoe-blade unless the few axeheads also served as such, so wooden digging sticks or mat-tocks must have been employed. The great majority of flint *Plates, 18, 19* tools are rough flakes or neat but monotonous parallel-sided blades, both to serve as knives. Scrapers for cleaning hides in preparation for making garments or other articles of leather are quite frequent. Leather must in fact have played an important part in the dress fashions of the time since evidence for spinning and weaving does not appear until the next period. Occasionally burins or gravers are found, chisel-shaped tools for working bone into pins, awls and spatulas.

The raw material from which these were fashioned was nearly always flint, which is common throughout the peninsula. However, obsidian is already occasionally found, showing that as early as this people were not limited solely to their local resources. It is a natural volcanic glass, black and shiny, and flakes more readily than flint. Since it does not occur in mainland Italy, the blades of it from prehistoric sites must have been imported from outside. The volcanic island of Lipari off the north coast of Sicily was much the most important of the sources and plays a prominent part in our story in consequence. So, despite the simple economy of the period, trade was already beginning to play a part, the goods being bartered from tribe to tribe. The main route of distribution seems to have been from Lipari to the Campanian coast by sea, then across the Ariano pass to the Tavoliere and on to the rest of Apulia.

Certain other goods were widely traded too. Suitable stone for grinding into axeheads is not found in the limestones of the peninsula between the Sila down in Calabria and northern Umbria. Trade in this also soon developed to supply the need. *Fig. 1* Even more remarkable, finds of Red on Buff pottery in Central Italy are so few yet so typical that they can hardly be local products. The demand for this fine ware must have been enormous for the difficulties of transporting it, for example to the Grotta Frasassi, to have been overcome. This cave is on the Sentino near Ancona, 80 difficult miles from the nearest known site *Plate 13, Fig. 45* where the ware is common. One wonders how many axeheads it would have cost at the end of its journey.

Plate 4

Plate 16

Although Apulia remained the centre of development throughout the period, as its population grew so new districts were colonised. Typical Molfetta and Red on Buff Wares were found on the site of La Starza, a rocky hillock controlling all traffic through the Ariano pass. The spread northwards is marked by finds of a variant form of Impressed Ware in the Marche and on into Emilia. From the type site of Ripabianca di Monterado near Ancona came vessels which had been given long ribs incorporating handles in addition to the normal Mol, fetta Ware features. Associated with this pottery were flint tools markedly different from the narrow knife-blades of the south. Broader flakes and burins in particular are much closer to Mesolithic or even Upper Palaeolithic forms. There was in this area apparently some fruitful contact between the incoming farmers and the native hunters, perhaps even intermarriage of the two peoples.

Southwards, colonising bands spread through Calabria and from there crossed to Sicily where their culture developed into that known as Stentinello after a ditched site near Syracuse. Sicily in turn became a centre from which the new ideas of food production were passed on by colonists to areas beyond: Malta, North Africa, Lipari, Liguria and Provence. Our interest in the story of the Italian peninsula must not obscure the fact that it is but one link in the chain connecting the ancient Near East with the furthermost parts of Europe.

What drove these farmers forward? With their primitive methods of agriculture, fully permanent settlements were impossible. Having moved into a new area and built themselves a village, they would fell and burn off sufficient scrub and tree cover to take the year's crops, hoe in the resulting ashes and dibble the seed corn into the ground. Next year and the year after the same plot would have its weeds cleared and burnt and another crop planted. Soon the soil's fertility would suffer, the crops would begin to fail and a new cycle would have to be begun on untouched land. Within a span of years – perhaps ten, perhaps thirty, depending on the fertility of the soil and the area cultivable – the virgin woodland within reach of the village would all have been used. The villagers would have no choice but to move on to a new site with fresh territory. The procedure can be studied today among primitive tribes in the tropical forests of Amazonia, for example, where this method is still practised.

The same factor, the area of good soil accessible from the village, would also limit its size. If the population rose above a certain size, the village would outgrow its fields and have to split by sending out a colony. Soil exhaustion and growing population between them provided the motive force for the spread of the Neolithic across Italy, as across the rest of Europe.

The vicious circle could be broken only by improved techniques of farming: like the use of heavier yielding corn, a simple crop rotation (or more likely crop alternation, corn and fallow), the use of manure from the domestic animals as a fertiliser and the deeper stirring of the soil made possible by the introduction of the plough. Any of these would permit a larger population and a longer-lived settlement. Unfortunately the plough is the only one which can leave a mark in the archaeological record, and, in a country like the Italian peninsula, even it is unlikely to do so. Here there are neither barrows to cover, and so 'fossil-ise', furrowed fields nor peat-bogs to preserve the ploughs themselves. Our first proof of the plough is a rock engraving dated tentatively to the Copper Age, to be described later (p. 76).

We are left with circumstantial evidence, but this is conclusive. How many and which of the agricultural improvements go back to the Middle Neolithic we may never know; the site of Passo di Corvo shows that some of them did, since its size and permanence could not have been achieved without. Plate 1, *Fig. 10*

Size was not the only difference in these later settlements. Over the whole of Southern Italy at this time the Red on Buff

Painted Ware remained popular, but everywhere the light-coloured and impressed Molfetta Ware went right out of fash-ion, to be replaced by dark burnished fabrics. The version of these to appear on the Tavoliere was undecorated and shaped into open dishes with flat bases and angled walls. With its plain surface it has attracted little study and until the excavations here are published its importance and relationships cannot be fairly judged.

At Ariano, in deposits slightly later than those with Molfetta Ware, a finer form of Impressed Ware appeared commonly, burnished inside and out and fired to a dark colour. On the open bowls, decoration was confined to impressed C's round *Fig. 11* the lip. The rocker pattern still occurred, reduced to a very narrow jagged line which was made the starting point for the development of the Matera Scratched Ware in the later Middle Neolithic. It is more gouged than impressed, being cut into the pot's surface with a short chisel-edge just before the pot was baked. Occasionally this was not done until after the firing, since on careful examination one can see that the hard but brittle burnished surface had flaked a little beneath the potter's flint graver. This ragged edge was obviously intentional, and now that the graver was producing it directly there was no longer any need of a to-and-fro motion, the point could be drawn straight across the surface. The purpose of this was to create a decoration of lines which could be picked out by an inlay of red ochre, the ragged edges providing the necessary key to hold the ochre in position.

It can best be explained as an ingenious way out of a difficul-ty. The increasingly popular dark burnished surface and the painted decoration which had not yet dropped out of favour could not be produced by the potters on a single ware. If the pot was baked in the oxygen-scarce atmosphere necessary to get the dark coloured surface, the paints available to them would also be dark and so barely visible. The decoration of scratches

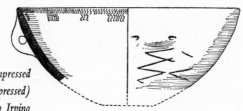

Fig. 11. Bowl with C-impressed design of Ariano (Late Impressed) Ware. La Starza, Ariano Irpino

and ochre applied after the firing produced the desired effect in a practical manner. About the same time in the south of France and a little later in Malta (the Chassey and Ġgantija Wares), the same solution was found to the same problem. In Malta indeed we have examples of the abortive attempts at dark-on-dark painted decoration immediately preceding the ochred scratches. The designs in the three wares are quite different and there is probably no connection between them. The Chassey pottery did have its effect on the Italian peninsula, as we shall see in the Final Neolithic.

A point to note with regard to the red ochre is that it would be rapidly removed by water. The vessels could therefore be cleaned only by wiping round inside. Possibly they were left dirty.

The decorative motifs produced in this technique were simple chequers, triangles and chevrons, which were perhaps fore-shadowed in some of the neater incised designs on Molfetta Impressed Ware. The dark burnish together with the scratched line derives directly from the Ariano version of Impressed Ware. The use of solid colour, achieved by filling areas with single or cross-hatching, owes more to the Red on Buff tradition. This is also apparent in the vessel shapes, the same globular and necked bowls, both with round bases and no handles. Clearly when the decorative limitations of Molfetta Ware ceased to satisfy the potters' creative urge, they built up a new and more versatile ware from the elements with which they were already familiar. Nor were they averse to mixing the different styles on

Fig. 12

47

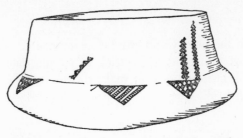

Fig. 12. Vaso a tocco, *Matera. (After Mayer)*

the same vessel. A very fine deep bowl from the Grotta Ostuni near Brindisi has not only a zone round its lip illustrating admirably the range of Matera Scratched designs, but also Molfetta rocker-patterning over its lower wall.

This ware takes its name from the city of Matera, around which occur a number of sites of this period. To the Grotta dei Pipistrelli already mentioned were added several ditched homesteads such as La Murgecchia, Murgia Timone and two at Tirlecchia. These are all placed high on a limestone escarpment with wide views across the clay lands to the north, where their cultivated fields lay, or down the gorge to the south, where their stock grazed. Serra d'Alto, better known for its Late Neolithic material, crowns a separate hill three miles to the north. They differ from the smaller Tavoliere homesteads only in their choice of country and the absence of the C-shaped compound ditches within the enclosure. A curious and unexplained detail occurring on sites in both areas confirms the connection, a short outward bulge of the ditch possibly forming some kind of entrance.

The Scratched Ware occurs frequently throughout eastern Lucania and the southern two-thirds of Apulia. It is common also at Ariano but surprisingly scarce on the Tavoliere, where only a few sherds are known. These were probably imported from surrounding areas and so provide useful synchronisms.

The material of the Middle Neolithic leaves the impression that this was a period of great prosperity. Support is given to this view by the size of the Tavoliere villages, the spread of farming communities throughout the southern and eastern regions of the peninsula and the great improvements, functional

Plate 17

Plate 3, *Fig. 9*

and artistic, made in the pottery. Shortly before 3500 B C – more radiocarbon determinations are needed to fix the date more closely – new influences begin to make themselves felt, to start a fresh chapter in the story.

LATE NEOLITHIC

There are no hard and fast divisions between the different periods of the Italian Neolithic. It is a story of continuous development, certain pottery styles coming into fashion as others, after a longer or shorter currency, gradually drop out. At no point can one see a sweeping change in the pottery even on a single site, still less over the whole peninsula.

This is in contrast to the situation revealed by the excavations on Lipari and Malta for example, islands which were too small for more than one style of pottery to flourish at a time. As a result, single unmixed levels there rarely contain sherds of more than one ware or at most two, one fine and one coarse. In the succeeding level these are replaced rapidly and completely without appreciable overlap. It was hoped that more careful work in the peninsula would be able to show a similar linear sequence of the many pottery wares known there. Instead, evidence is accumulating from many recently studied sites, such as Bolognano, Ariano and the Tavoliere villages, that the apparent mixtures were genuine associations, that the sherds are found together simply because they were lost together. Indeed it is not uncommon to find that the local potters were making three or four different and quite distinct wares at any one time, and in addition vessels of perhaps as many more wares were being imported from neighbouring areas.

The implication of this is that there was a great deal of coming and going. Whereas the Middle Neolithic Red on Buff Ware had been traded north to the Marche and south to Calabria, Serra d'Alto Ware of the Late Neolithic is found as far afield as Tuscany and Malta. Trade was becoming an ever more important factor, not only by raising the standard of living but also by making possible the rapid spread of new ideas. Styles of pottery are a comparatively unimportant example of this; others of more significance will be discussed shortly.

A second and less fortunate implication is that it is almost impossible to divide the Neolithic period into neat stages except in a purely arbitrary fashion; the changes are much too gradual and take some time to make themselves felt throughout the peninsula. We took the introduction of the Red on Buff Ware as the criterion of the Middle Neolithic. The Late Neolithic is marked by the appearance of three new painted wares, named after the sites of Capri, Ripoli and Serra d'Alto. However, we cannot assume that all three arrived instantaneously, that their spread from their points of entry was at a uniform rate, and that the wares they replaced disappeared immediately everywhere. There is some evidence to the contrary, emphasising that the division, though convenient, is artificial.

The Capri and Ripoli Wares have many features in common and may be regarded as variant forms of a single imported pottery style. If so, Ripoli is the earlier in origin since it is much closer in appearance to the ancestral painted ware found at Danilo in Dalmatia. On the other hand, there is a good deal to suggest that its painted ware survived in use well into the Final Neolithic, by which time the Capri Ware had already dropped out of fashion. Since the site of Ripoli is within 4 miles of the Adriatic coast, at the northern edge of the Abruzzi, it may represent the point of arrival of this pottery tradition in Italy.

Both wares are characterised by a buff fabric rather softer than that of the Red on Buff Ware, and by the use of black and red paint together. On the Ripoli Ware, thin black lines form panels of geometric hatched designs enclosed within a band consisting of a row of dots between two parallel lines. The rest of the

Fig. 13

Fig. 13. Vessels of Capri Flame, Capri Buff and Ripoli Painted Wares. The red paint is represented by dotting. From the Castello di Lipari, the Grotta delle Felci and Ripoli. (After Brea and Rellini)

surface was then given a wash of red paint, on which the panels appear to float. Decorated in this manner were baggy cups with round bases and small clumsy handles. Many of the handles are surmounted by a knob which seems to have fired the potters' imagination. They developed it into an elaborate projection, forked at the tip and decorated with subsidiary knobs. In one example at least it has become a recognisable human figure, with a flat body and head, arms and breasts all roughly indicated.

Fig. 14

Fig. 14. Handles of Figulina Ware, Ripoli

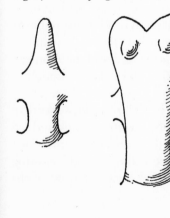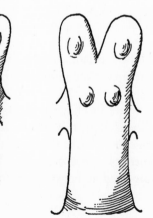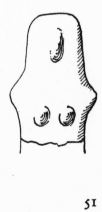

51

This is the first time we meet a phenomenon which lasts throughout Italian prehistory: the fascination which handles seem to have held for the potters of the peninsula. Their use of surface decoration, impressed, painted or incised, is often attractive but rarely outstanding in comparison with that ornamenting pottery elsewhere in Europe at the time. But nowhere else was so much emphasis placed on three-dimensional moulding of the handles. At Ripoli there is little artistry to be seen in the results, which can only be described as quaint. At Serra d'Alto, in the Apennine Bronze Age, and again in the Daunian Iron Age, to name only three examples, the handles become fantastic and at times strangely beautiful. And yet one can rarely see any connecting link between these wares; it is a phenomenon, not simply a tradition.

Plates 27, 28
Plates 63, 65

Ripoli itself is the best known of a number of prehistoric settlements on the terraces of the Vibrata Valley. It comprised a number of hut foundations like those of Penne. Even more numerous were smaller and deeper pits now regarded as grain storage silos. When they became too musty for grain, they were used as rubbish dumps or even on occasion for human burial. In one was discovered the crouched skeleton of a man with his dog lying at his feet. A recent re-excavation has shown that the village was surrounded by a ditch. It yielded rich material which, when published, may help to clarify the history of this long-lived site. To take two examples, many finely worked arrowheads and evidence of weaving in the shape of spindle whorls and discoid loom-weights have come from Ripoli. The former are not known elsewhere before the Final Neolithic and the latter are not closely dated anywhere. Until we have stratified or otherwise unmixed groups of material, we cannot tell at what period of the village's life these advances in the arts of war and peace made their appearance.

Characteristic Ripoli Painted Ware is found widely scattered over the upper half of the peninsula from Capri to Liguria, so far in such small quantity that it may have been traded from centres of production in the Abruzzi. A related ware, known by the Italian name of *figulina,* is equally widespread and much more frequent. It is a buff ware so soft that it rarely survives except as small sherds, of which the surface has often decayed. Occasionally traces of paint remain to suggest that this material may be no more than poorly preserved Ripoli Ware. A radio-carbon reading from a deposit containing *figulina* sherds at Petescia, near Rieti, gave a date of 3450 ± 145 B C.

The Neolithic level in the Grotta delle Felci (the Cave of the Ferns; it was re-occupied in the Bronze Age) on the island of Capri contained the second of these painted wares. It differs from Ripoli Ware only in details – the dotted band does not appear, the red painted areas play a less important part in the design, the cups often have an angle between wall and round base and are not provided with handles. In its commonest form it is found widely over Southern Italy. A version in which the fabric is of a much higher quality, red and almost metallic, has not been recognised outside Capri itself. A third variety comes from Capri, Lipari and possibly some of the coastal sites be-tween them such as Praia. One sherd is known from the Pulo di Molfetta. In this the red bands are treated as motifs in their own right, sinuous and flame-like. On Lipari, small three-handled jars as well as the more usual cups of this Capri Flame Ware are known.

Plates 29–32
Fig. 13

Fig. 15. Pebbles painted in red with anthropomorphic? figures. Grotta del-le Felci, Capri. (After Buchner)

 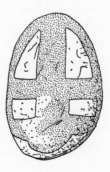 

Fig. 15

In the Grotta delle Felci were discovered some curious round-ed beach pebbles painted with bands of red. Resemblances to the Mesolithic painted pebbles of the Mas d'Azil in the French Pyrenees are probably coincidental. Stylised human figures have been recognised in some. They may have served some such purpose as the *churingas*, the sacred stone, bone or wooden objects of the Australian aborigines, which are linked in an obscure mesh of belief with myths, spirits and totems. They provide a tantalising testimony of the wide fields of pre-historic life which we can never hope to open up.

Fig. 9

Plates 25, 26

Easily the most attractive Neolithic pottery in Italy is the ware named after Serra d'Alto, an isolated hill 3 miles north of Matera. A village founded here in the preceding period flourished throughout the Late Neolithic and beyond. From its hut foundations and silo pits came a great quantity of a thin, hard, buff ware bearing designs either in black or more com-monly in dark purple-brown paint. These designs are not easy to summarise since, in contrast to all the painted wares so far described, they are extremely variable. To say that they are built up largely of neat rectangular meanders, frequently placed di-agonally, contrasting with small solid triangles, and with the bordered zigzag a very common secondary motif, is accurate but does the style less than justice. On every vessel in fact the potter used these motifs in a different way, adding related new ones or leaving out old ones as fancy directed, but always clearly retaining the over-all style. Even quite small sherds are unmis-takable. The originality and neatness shown by its creators give it exceptional charm.

Plate 26

The vessels so decorated are pleasing in their own right. The basic shape is a more or less globular body on which is set a straight neck or lip. Considerable variety is produced by vary-ing the heights and proportions of the two parts or by altering the slope of the neck. An open body with a low neck and single handle gives a cup form; a deeper body, higher neck and

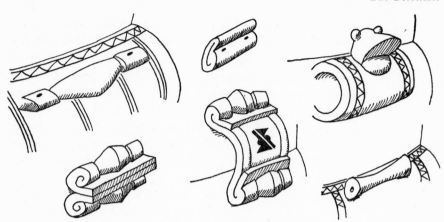

Fig. 16. Handles of Serra d' Alto Ware from various sites

two handles, a jar. The result is always a harmonious balance of the two elements, the curve and the line.

Plate 25

At Serra d'Alto as at Ripoli the painted decoration did not exhaust the inventiveness of the Late Neolithic potters. The handles gave an excuse for experimentation with three-dimensional subjects. On the jars, the broad, simple strap handles were first bent to run a short distance up the wall, so giving a firmer attachment. The idea was soon developed decoratively. The bent portion was doubled back on itself, then back again, or folded into itself, or humped into an ornamental triple knob. Similar treatment of lugs produced first one of ear-shaped section, then an S-shaped one and finally the most extraordinary folded and convoluted affairs like elaborately pleated table napkins or the Italian *pane al olio* rolls. The most famous of these is from Paternò in Sicily. The folded-back end is characteristic, if simple; the triple knob, comprising a large convex central element between two lower and flatter side ones, is absolutely unmistakable. But again the variations on these two basic themes are incredibly diverse.

Fig. 16

A different class of handle appears on the cups, basically long and tubular and always O- rather than D-shaped in section. Its centre is often surmounted by a knob modelled into a vaguely zoomorphic form. Sometimes it is sheep- or cow-like, sometimes duck- or frog-like, often some strange combination of two or more of these, like the duck-billed ram (or ram-horned duck) from Setteponti and the jousting helmet from the Scoglio del Tonno. The only known human representation appears on a notable open bowl from the type site which stands on two well-modelled human feet.

Plate 27
Plate 28

Serra d'Alto Ware was understandably popular, being traded or copied throughout much of Southern Italy, Sicily and beyond. Its origins, though obscure, must lie east of the Adriatic, where the meander motif has a long history. Sherds of it, as mentioned above, have been found in Tuscany in the north and Malta in the south, where it was associated with a radiocarbon date of 3225 ± 150 B C. It is particularly common around Matera and Taranto, where its makers founded the first settlement on the famous site of the Scoglio del Tonno.

Fig. 39

By contrast it has so far been found at only one of the Tavoliere villages, and even there in a very small quantity. To all appearances that densely populated area was abandoned at the end of the Middle Neolithic and apart from occasional visitors remained deserted until the later Iron Age. The reason must lie in climatic changes, which have so far been little studied. It is now the driest corner of Italy and through the summer months completely arid. Water is brought by long aqueducts from the mountains or pumped up from deep wells to make life possible. Yet many extinct water-courses can be traced on the air photographs and the density of Middle Neolithic occupation implies that they were still flowing streams then. In the Late Neolithic the only known sites in the district are off the Tavoliere itself, at Scaloria on the slopes of the Gargano, Arinao back among the Apennines and Canne (subsequently the scene of Hannibal's victory over Rome) beyond the River Ofanto, the largest in Apulia. As the water failed, so the villages and fields would have to be abandoned: man can adapt himself to a wide range of environments but water he cannot do without.

One other painted ware merits at least passing mention. Amongst the many varieties of pottery from the Grotta Scaloria were some cups of Serra d'Alto shape and with designs based on Serra d'Alto meanders, but they were painted in broad red bands, more like those of the Red on Buff Ware, bordered in black in the style of Capri. It was probably an experimental fusion of the three traditions and never achieved wide popularity. The only other site from which it has been recorded is the Grotta dell'Erba (the Cave of the Grass) at Avetrana, whence came a fine cup of identical shape and decorative technique. The main design is a striking asymmetric and abstract figure. A bordered zigzag inside its lip clinches the connection with the Serra d'Alto Ware.

Plate 23

Plate 24

The same site yielded a particularly fine example of a *pintadera,* a curious small patterned stamp of terracotta. These are believed to have been used for applying coloured designs to the human skin, an alternative to the more permanent and painful technique of tattooing. They are commoner in Northern Italy but occur sporadically in the south, where their designs are often related to Serra d'Alto motifs.

Fig. 17. Pintadera from the Grotta dell'Erba, Avetrana

While these developments were taking place in the south and east of the peninsula, the colonisation of the north and west was completed in the Late Neolithic. The site of Petescia has already been mentioned for its Figulina Ware and its radiocarbon date. Its material was not rich and suggests a small band of settlers who had pushed through the mountains to this open valley on the western slope. There is no trace here of fine painted wares or sophisticated handles. A coarse unburnished ware with finger-indented cordons as its only ornament also occurred, but most of the pottery was completely undistinguished. Handles all took the form of small tubular lugs splaying at the ends in a manner which became widely popular in the Final Neolithic. Further work is badly needed on the rougher and undecorated wares which have tended to receive less than their fair share of attention from archaeologists.

The coarse cordoned ware is found widely in the north-west and can best be named after the Grotta all'Onda (the Cave by the Stream) in the Alpi Apuane north of Pisa. This ware was so simple and serviceable that it remained in general use for cooking not only through the rest of the Neolithic but with little change throughout the Copper and Bronze Ages. It really disappeared only when pottery-making ceased to be a household chore for the women with the spread of professional craftsmen using the potter's wheel in the later Iron Age.

In this part of Italy another element has to be taken into consideration. The *pintaderas* in the south have already hinted at influence from the Po Valley. That area had been settled by Neolithic farmers moving up both shores of the Adriatic, some of whom had then been attracted southwards across the mountains by the empty countryside of Tuscany. Pottery very similar to that found at villages in Emilia (Fiorano Modenese provides the type site) comes from several cave sites in Tuscany and Latium, namely the Grotta dell'Orso (the Bear's Cave) at Sarteano, the Grotta Lattaia (Milkmaid Cave) at Cetona nearby, and particularly the Grotta Fabrizi (the name of the owner) at Sasso di Furbara near Rome. Sherds from other sites, Asciano near Pisa, Luni not far from Sasso, and Ripoli itself, show that the newcomers from the north had an even wider influence. A radiocarbon date of 3445 ± 80 from Luni is so close to that from Petescia, 3450, that the pioneering movements from north and east must be regarded as contemporaneous.

The Grotta Fabrizi was the richest of these sites, a natural cave used for burials. With the bones lay a number of cups

Plate 36

58

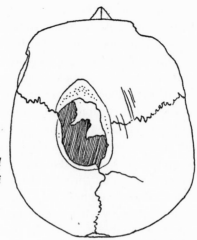

Fig. 18. Vertical view of the trepanned skull from the Grotta Fabrizi, Sasso di Furbara. (After Radmilli)

with straight necks, round bases and large plain handles. They had been burnished and decorated with broad grooved lines forming double chevrons or loops, in some of which traces of a crimson cinnabar inlay, derived from natural mercuric sulphide, survived. Larger ovoid or carinated jars were each provided with four handles and could also be decorated. Many objects of bone were recovered too, such as awls, some large enough to be used as spearheads, spatulas, perforated pendants and cannon bones with scratched cross or herringbone decoration of unknown use. Among the flint tools occurred obliquely blunted blades and end-scrapers. Hare and deer bones implied some reliance on hunting, but a number of querns proved that agriculture was the main basis of the economy.

Plate 35

Fig. 36

The most interesting interment was of a middle-aged man of some importance. He had been buried in an extended position against the back wall of the cave surrounded by a half-circle of stones and numerous grave goods. A number of anomalies were noticed in the proportions of his bones, suggesting some physical abnormality. Further, the skull had been trepanned, a

Fig. 18

delicate operation by which a disc of bone is removed to reveal the brain surface. The scratch marks of the flint surgical tool are still visible beside the opening. It is tempting to suppose that the dead man's abnormalities were mental as well as phy,sical, explaining perhaps the source of his importance, the re,spect and fear of primitive man for mental imbalance. Even more likely is that this was the reason for the operation, to re,lease the 'evil spirit'. Here trepanning was not only more pain,ful than a psychiatrist's couch, it was less effective. The absence of healing in the bone showed that the patient did not survive his operation.

FINAL NEOLITHIC

The Italian Neolithic does not fall neatly into the traditional threefold divisions of Early, Middle and Late, but rather into four. Since the last of these begins to show cultural elements more proper to the succeeding Copper Age but is too impor, tant in its own right to be dismissed as a mere transitional phase, the name of Final Neolithic seems appropriate. It is a period in which the peninsula is affected less from the east, as previously, but profoundly from the south,west and north,west, a reflux movement of influence following the primary colonisations of those areas. To understand this movement we must consider developments elsewhere in the West Mediterranean.

In Sicily one descendant of the Impressed Ware stock, if one may describe pottery styles in such biological terms, had pro,duced by the Late Neolithic a fine undecorated ware charac,terised by a bright red slip and splayed tubular handles. Marmo on the slope of Mount Etna provides a convenient type site. A related development, with similar slip and handles, has been fully documented at Skorba in Malta, where according to the radiocarbon dates it was completed by 3200 B C. The name usually applied to this group of wares is Diana, from the Neo, lithic village extending at the foot of the citadel of Lipari. There Diana Ware, closely related to Marmo, was stratified above, and completely replaced, Serra d'Alto Ware. Though its origins lay south of Lipari, its later development could be followed in higher levels. The splayed handles were made progressively longer and lower, soon becoming imperforate and non-functional, the so-called trumpet lugs. A short, angled lip to the vessels was also characteristic.

When pottery with the same three features of slip, lip and lug was noted on the mainland, it was assumed to be identical with the Diana Ware of Lipari and necessarily later than Serra d'Alto Ware in consequence. Recent discoveries lead one to question both conclusions. Sherds of undoubted Diana Ware have been discovered on sites facing Lipari across the lower Tyrrhenian Sea, probably exchanged by obsidian traders or fishermen. At Praia they were claimed to come from a level overlying Serra d'Alto material but both levels were poor; full publication is awaited. Inland, however, the three characteristics of Diana Ware, though present, are never found all together on single vessels nor even on single sites.

The most distinctive, the red slip, has so far been recorded only from Ariano and the caves of the Fucino, at the Grotta Maritza with a saddled lug but on the other sites without either the lug or the angled lip. Tombs at Girifalco near Catanzaro and the Masseria Bellavista at Taranto, consisting of hollows cut in the rock to take crouched burials, yielded a few vessels with out-turned lips and saddled lugs but in a soft grey ware quite unlike that of Diana. The handles too are much less exaggerated than the trumpet lugs of Lipari. Similar pots have been found occasionally elsewhere in the south. A second vessel from Bellavista was of the same ware and with identical handles but had a simple lip and an extraordinary pouch-shaped strainer spout. It may have been used for drinking an infusion of leaves, a practice which goes back long before tea was imported into

Fig. 29

Fig. 39, Plate 34

Plate 33

Europe. Apart from the spout, this type of vessel is a great deal commoner.

Fig. 39

A useful grave group came from the fifth of six stone-built cist graves outside the Scoglio del Tonno a few miles away. It comprised four small jars of the same shape though without spouts, a low straight-walled dish and a small carinated bowl. All but one of the jars had saddled lugs. A blade of Lipari obsidian and a polished greenstone axe amulet perhaps from the Sila completed the tally, together with the skeleton of their former owner. One cannot unfortunately use this as the type site of this ware because the Scoglio del Tonno is so much better known for its Bronze Age material. Although slightly less satisfactory, the name of Bellavista Ware will be used instead.

Various forms of splayed and saddled lugs occur in other fabrics throughout much of the peninsula at this time. They have already been noted at Petescia, for example. At Norcia in Umbria a rather coarse ware with large pale grits and lugs with their ends expanded into spikes rather than trumpets was the standard ware in a village of huts surviving as shallow pits in the ground. The same ware and handles have been found at Ripoli and a number of sites in the Marche.

What do these facts mean? Clearly these wares, from Malta to the Marche, are a number of separate local groups and although the Diana style of Lipari was to some extent copied by potters of the mainland (the everted lipped vessels and the red slip), it would be most misleading to regard all these groups as variations of a single widespread ware. Until it is proved that the fashion for splayed lugs was due to borrowing from tribe to tribe rather than an independent development in different areas, it would be better not to try to apply a single collective name to them all, particularly not a name like Diana which already has distinctive characteristics in one special group, that on Lipari.

Before leaving the south, it must be stressed that the increase in importance of various undecorated wares does not imply the

disappearance of pottery painting. At both the Grotta La Punʹ
ta in the Fucino basin and at Ariano, typical Serra d'Alto *Fig. 29*, Plate 4
sherds were found associated with Diana (red slipped) and
Bellavista ones, showing that the painted ware still survived in
use. More interestingly, a later version of Serra d'Alto Ware
has been recognised, showing signs of Diana contact. Some of
the silo pits in the Gravela property on the hill of Serra d'Alto
contained pottery which differed from the standard painted
ware in several respects. The fabric remains very much the same
but the profiles become either taut and fussy or loose and baggy;
the decoration is reduced to a sparing use of the bordered zigʹ
zag, often no more than a finicky edging like an illʹconsidered
strip of lace; and the fanciful handles are replaced by uniform,
thin, splayed, tubular lugs. These are unlike anything found *Fig. 16*
in Serra d'Alto Ware earlier but are strikingly similar to those
of later Diana Ware, from which they must have been derived.
They demonstrate alike the contemporaneity or at least overlap
of the two wares and the decline in the artistic skill of the Serra
d'Alto potters.

Turning to the north, we have to take at least a rapid look
even farther afield. Various Neolithic cultures in Western Eurʹ
ope have been classed as a single family known simply as the
Western Neolithic. The earliest of these is the Chassey Culture
of Central France, with radiocarbon dates well before 3000
BC. Of its origins little is known. Derivation from the Imʹ
pressed Ware of Provence, itself derived from Stentinello in
Sicily, has been suggested. Another possibility is an origin in
the Almerian Culture of southern Spain. This in turn has
roots in the Impressed Ware Culture of North Africa, which
could be either another Stentinello derivative by way of Tunisia
or a separate group coming direct from the Nile valley across
what is now the Sahara. This sketchy outline should be suffiʹ
cient to show that however vague the details of the story in
Italy, it is much clearer than in many neighbouring areas.

The only member of the Western Neolithic family to concern the Italian peninsula is that called after the site of Lagozza di Besnate near Brescia in the north. This was one of a number of *palafitte* or pile settlements by the swampy rivers of the Po valley and the North Italian lakes. The culture was established during the Late Neolithic as here defined, and flourished for some considerable time. There is a radiocarbon date of 2845 ± 90 B C from Lagozza itself. The distinctive pile villages naturally occur only in suitable environments. Their charac- teristic pottery and other material are found also in caves and open settlements on dry land. The ware is highly burnished, black and undecorated, and was shaped most frequently into baggy or carinated cups and jars with rounded bases, or straight- walled open dishes. Handles are unknown but knobs perforat- ed to take a loop of cord to serve instead are very common. These lugs may occur in pairs or even occasionally in multiple form like a strip of corrugated cardboard attached to the pot. This is a type found also in Chassey Ware, where it is known as a *flute de Pan* or Pan-pipe handle. Scratched decoration, as at Chassey, appears only in hatched triangles inside the lips of saucers.

These were mainly a farming people but it is unlikely that they disregarded completely the fish and molluscs of the rivers and lakes by which they lived. Arrowheads, always of the *Fig. 20e* chisel-edged form, with a cutting edge rather than a point, also suggest wild-fowling, since it is easier to break a bird's wing with one of these than it is to transfix it outright. Important innovations are spinning and weaving, attested by flat spindle whorls and conical loom weights of terracotta. Bone combs found at Lagozza may have been used for cloth-making, to prepare the fibres for spinning or to compact the wefts on the loom. Pebbles with scratched cross-hatching remain an enigma.

Material of Lagozza type had been found at Ripoli as long ago as 1912 but only in the last few years has the importance of

Fig. 19. Vessels of Lagozza Ware from the Grotta dei Piccioni, Bolognano

this culture in the peninsula been recognised. The ware is common and fully represented in caves near Pisa (from one of which came a second trepanned skull) but does not penetrate far on this side of the peninsula. There is a single sherd from Belverde. On the Adriatic slope it appears in quantity and characteristic form at sites in the Marche like Santa Maria in Selva and Attigio di Fabriano. At Ripoli black burnished and carinated bowls and vases with rolled rims and internal handles are clearly related. It by-passes the Fucino sites but reappears in rather simpler form at Bolognano. Here it forms the bulk of the large quantity of material excavated by A. M. Radmilli in the latest Neolithic level, being associated with Serra d'Alto and Ripoli Painted Wares and with a radiocarbon date of 2820 ± 110 BC. Some intriguing circular settings of stones containing three disarticulated children's skeletons give another hint of ritual practices. At Ariano this ware accounted for over 13 feet of deposit. One characteristic sherd from the Pulo di Molfetta and scratched pebbles from Monopoli beyond Bari, probably related to it, carry the story even further south.

Plate 11

Fig. 19

Plate 4
Plate 2

Whereas traits from the Diana Culture found in the peninsula can be interpreted as evidence for sporadic conracts only,
probably through the obsidian trade, the Lagozza Culture,
being represented by a complete range of its pottery types and
by other objects such as spindle whorls, loom weights, chisel-
ended arrowheads and occasionally scratched pebbles, must be
due to a movement of people down the eastern side of the
peninsula. The association of wares at Ripoli and Bolognano
shows that the change-over was neither complete nor violent.
Indeed, the widespread Ripoli Studded Ware seems to be due
to fusion between the local and immigrant traditions. It is of a
soft pinkish fabric resembling that of the Ripoli Painted or
Figulina Wares, modelled into carinated dishes of Lagozza
shape and distinguished from both by a decoration of studs
around the neck. Nor is this the only hybrid ware at Ripoli. The
second has the pale gritty fabric of Norcia Ware forming baggy
cups with knobbed handles, as in Ripoli Painted Ware, set on
pedestals unlike either. These tulip-shaped vessels are not found
outside the Vibrata valley.

The late dating of these wares is confirmed by artifacts of
other materials found with them. Firstly, until this stage of the
Neolithic, arrowheads were practically unknown in the peninsula. Either untipped arrows and spears were used for hunting,
or more likely the sling was the basic weapon; there are probable
sling stones from Italian sites and unquestioned ones in neighbouring areas. On Final Neolithic sites arrowheads appear in
Fig. 20 quantity and great variety, chisel-ended, leaf-shaped, hollow-
based and in particular a wide range of barbed and tanged
forms, in the upper level at Bolognano for example, at Ariano, Ripoli, Norcia and many of the sites in the Marche. At
Serra d'Alto one was found with sherds of the later version of
that ware, but they are on the whole less frequent in the south.

Wild animal bones from sites of this period, red and roe
deer, at Norcia even otter, suggest the use to which some of

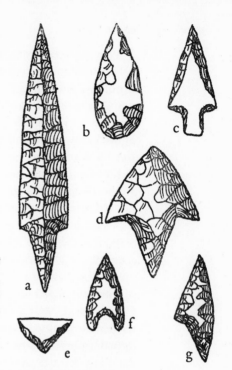

Fig. 20 Final Neolithic and Copper Age flint arrowheads. From Casamari (barbed and tanged, a), Ariano (leaf-shaped, b), Rinaldone, Conelle (both barbed and tanged, c, d), Ariano (transverse and hollow-based, e, f) and Ripoli (single barbed, g)

these arrows were put. It has already been mentioned that the chisel-ended arrows seem to have been designed for shooting birds. But the finding of stone maceheads and axe-hammers in the Marche and even down at Girifalco in Calabria points to warfare as well as hunting having by now appeared. The defensive ditch recently identified at Ripoli carries similar implications. We are in fact on the verge of a period of unrest which coincides roughly with the time span of the Copper Age.

Similarly, the appearance of spinning and weaving cannot be securely dated before this time. Although loom weights found at Ripoli, in the Fucino basin and at Ariano are not of the same form as those at Lagozza, being large and disc-shaped rather than conical, this movement of settlers from the north seems the likeliest moment for the techniques of textile-making to have been introduced into the peninsula.

An even more important innovation was the appearance of the first metal. On Lipari, traces of copper-smelting have been found in the late Diana levels. Scraps of copper came from the two sites in the Marche already mentioned, Santa Maria in Selva and Attigio, where they were found with Lagozza material, including a fine Pan-pipe lug, together with Ripoli Studded and Norcia Wares and a variety of arrowheads. Although formally Neolithic, these people were gradually learning of the discoveries of metallurgy made elsewhere. In time their cultures and wares were replaced by those of the full Copper Age.

Plate 4

A rather different situation was found at Ariano. The level containing Serra d'Alto, Bellavista and Diana material was covered by a 13 foot-thick rich deposit of pure but late and simple Lagozza type. Near the middle of this was found a copper awl together with imported sherds of the undoubted Copper Age Wares of Piano Conte and Conelle, to be described in the next chapter. At the very top, the Lagozza Ware turned imperceptibly into Apennine Ware, characteristic of the Early Bronze Age. Here the Neolithic Lagozza Culture survived, almost but not quite untouched by the upheavals of the Copper Age, to play a major part in the formation of the brilliant Apennine Culture at a later date. Yet only a few years ago it was not realised that the Lagozza Culture had entered the peninsula at all.

CHAPTER IV

The Copper Age

THE APPEARANCE in any area of new techniques of econ-omy or manufacture, new pottery styles or tool types, new shapes of huts or villages, new burial rites or religious beliefs, new spoken languages or written scripts, can be explained in many different ways: they may be due to local development, to political, commercial or religious influence from outside, or to the actual immigration of people who had learnt them elsewhere, and it is often far from easy to determine which. If, however, the men themselves change suddenly, as shown by the form of their skeletons, this can be explained only by immigration. Apart from such minor alterations as dyeing of the hair, tat-tooing of the skin, filing or extracting of the teeth, man has less control over his own person than over any other of his posses-sions. When, therefore, we find that tombs of the Italian Copper Age contain skeletons with markedly round skulls, which were virtually unknown during the Neolithic, we know that new peoples have moved into the country. We may further assume, though not prove, that the many other innovations at this time were introduced by these newcomers.

This immediately raises the problem of whence the immi-grants came, to which no firm answer can yet be given. Of the several distinguishable cultural groups in the peninsula, some show traits which point to Central Europe, others suggest contact with the Aegean, yet others share characteristics with both regions, leaving a few which seem to be native and un-affected by the new ideas.

A clear example of the first of these is provided by the Re-medello Culture, the home of which, though outside the pen-insula, was close enough to have some influence on the area we are primarily concerned with. A few settlement sites and

REMEDELLO

Fig. 21

a number of quite large cemeteries have been found in the middle valley of the Po, on both banks of the river. The simple trench graves contained crouched skeletons, a proportion of them round-headed, accompanied by the personal possessions of the deceased.

Fig. 42

Fig. 23

Much the most important finds were the objects of metal. They included flat axes of the simplest type, angular daggers with a midrib, tang and single rivet, and awls of square section. There is no natural copper in this area, and recent analyses have shown that extensive trade relations brought it in from several distinct sources. One of these was in central Germany or Bohemia since some tools were found to contain traces of nickel, as in the copper ores of those regions. Others may eventually be identified as the products of southern Tuscan, Sardinian and Austrian deposits. A pin with a T-shaped head and a crescentic ornamental plate of silver were also found, these too of Bohemian origin. The shape of the daggers is less easy to explain, the closest parallels being in Early Minoan Crete.

Fig. 20

Finely pressure-flaked barbed and tanged arrowheads were frequent. Beads and buttons of various substances, with straight converging holes making V-perforations, were employed for

Fig. 42

personal adornment. Pottery was scarce in the tombs but was found more commonly on the domestic sites. Most notable are some sherds of Beaker Ware, which was diffused throughout much of Europe by the first traders in metal.

This culture is clearly the result of immigration across the Alps, probably by way of the Brenner Pass. The copper and silver, the Beaker sherds and the round-headed skulls all point in that direction. The metal types are less informative than one might hope. The axes and awls are of forms too simple and generalised to be of much help. The tanged daggers, if not imports from the Aegean, must have been a local development.

Two sites in the peninsula show Remedello influence. At Vecchiano near Lucca a typical dagger was found together

Fig. 21 Copy Age sites and regions

1. Menhirs of the Lunigiana
2. Alpi Apuane (Grotta all'Onda, Vecchiano, etc.)
3. Monte Bradoni, Volterra
4. Pianosa
5. Pomarance
6. Belverde di Cetona
7. Fiora valley (Ponte San Pietro, Garavicchio, Montemerano, etc.)
8. Rinaldone, Montefiascone
9. Luni
10. Cantalupo Mandela
11. Sgurgola
12. Casamari, Frosinone
13. Palmarola, Pontine Islands
14. Vescovaro, Osimo
15. Conelle di Arcevia
16. Fucino (Ortucchio, etc.) See Fig. 29
17. Ripoli, Vibrata
18. Grotta dei Piccioni, Bolognano
19. La Starza, Ariano Irpino
20. Grotta delle Felci, Capri
21. Rione Mattadei, Naples
22. Mirabella Eclano
23. Gaudo, Paestum
24. Gargano (Tagliacantone, Macchia a Mare, etc.)
25. Castelluccio de' Sauri
26. Andria
27. Altamura
28. Gioia del Colle
29. Grotta Ostuni
30. Crispiano, Taranto. See Fig. 39
31. San Vito dei Normanni
32. Cellino San Marco
33. Santa Maria al Bagno, Nardò
34. Vanze, Lecce
35. Otranto (Minervino, Giurdignano, etc.)
36. Grotta Sant'Angelo, Cassano
37. Morano Calabro
38. Grotta della Madonna, Praia
39. Roggiano Gravina
40. Lipari (Castello, Piano Conte, etc.)

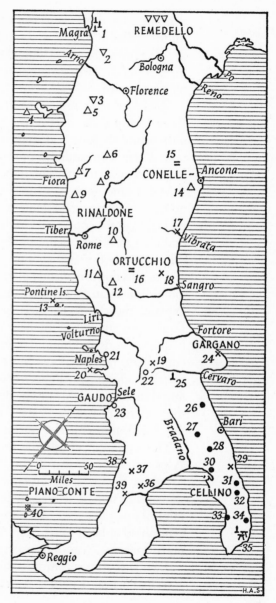

71

with 31 barbed and tanged arrowheads, local Grotta all'Onda Ware (see p. 58) and a large number of skeletons in a natural cave. The dagger probably arrived by trade, possibly in ex/ change for marble from the Alpi Apuane for making into beads. Another burial cave, at Monte Bradoni, Volterra, yield/ ed four Remedello daggers. They were of Bohemian copper, a surprising fact considering the nearness of the Tuscan ores, and might imply a party of prospectors in search of metal supplies. Three V/perforated buttons from this site were at first thought to be of tin, with important implications for the appearance of bronze in this area, but when analysed they proved to be of antimony, which is found locally.

RINALDONE Southward from the Remedello province, the territory of a second cultural group extended over most of Tuscany, Umbria and Latium, with outlying sites in neighbouring regions. A/ part from a possible settlement at Luni, where a few sherds were found in the open, the evidence at present comes solely from tombs and for that reason has its limitations. Many of these tombs are trench graves like those of Remedello, including the

Plate 37 nine which make up the type site, Rinaldone near Montefias/
Plate 11 cone, Viterbo. Natural caves, as at Belverde, and stone/built cists were also occasionally used. In three districts, the island of Pianosa, the valley of the River Fiora on the borders between Tuscany and Latium, and in the hills east of Rome, special chambers were cut in the rock to receive the dead.

One tomb from a cemetery excavated in a bank of soft volcan/
Plate 5 ic tuff above the Fiora at Ponte San Pietro has been chosen for detailed description to serve as an example. It can now be seen
Fig. 22 restored at the new Pigorini Museum in Rome. Its oval chamber measured 7 feet 9 inches by 6 feet 8 and was only 2 feet 3 inches high. The entrance, sealed with a slab of rock, opened onto the slope.

To the right of the doorway lay the crouched skeleton of a middle/aged man, his legs loosely bent and his hands close to

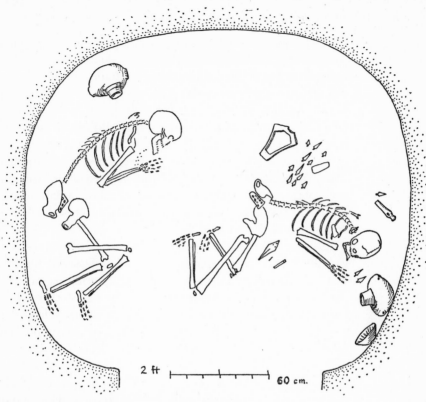

Fig. 22. Tomb of the Widow (no. 14), Ponte San Pietro

the face. Against the wall above his head were a *bottiglia* (a
globular jar with cylindrical neck and partly recessed handles)
and a deep dish having alternating groups of straight and wavy
pattern‚burnished lines on its inner dark polished surface. Be‚
hind the skeleton's head was a fine polished battle‚axe having
a knob at one end, an axe edge at the other and a hole for haft‚
ing at the centre. Three barbed and tanged flint arrowheads
were placed near it. Below his elbows lay a copper dagger with
triangular blade and base, the latter having three rivets in a deep
V‚formation but no sign of the presumably wooden hilt. With

Fig. 24a

Fig. 20a
Fig. 23c

73

the dagger were a hone for sharpening it, consisting of a small bar of sandstone with a perforation at one end, and a copper awl point, whose handle had likewise disappeared. Behind his back twelve more arrowheads were carefully laid out between a flat copper axe and a curious object cut from a broad deer antler and hollowed to form a receptacle, perhaps for paint.

Against the wall to the left of the entrance lay a second skeleton in an identical position. It was of a young adult woman and showed signs of injury to the skull. Her only possessions were another *bottiglia* and the remains of a bead necklace. The woman's skeleton gives the tomb its name of the Tomb of the Widow, the assumption being that it illustrates the rite of *sati*, by which a wife is despatched to accompany her husband into the after-life, implying amongst other things a patriarchal society. It may well do so, but many other interpretations of the archaeological evidence are possible. The woman may equally well have predeceased her husband by many years, after an accident with a falling branch. Or the two may be mother and son, or completely unrelated by marriage or blood.

Fig. 23. Copper Age daggers and halberds. From left to right, Monte Bradoni (Remedello type), Rinaldone tomb 3, Guardistallo, Pomarance (8½ inches long, first three to the same scale) and Roggiano Gravina (13 inches long)

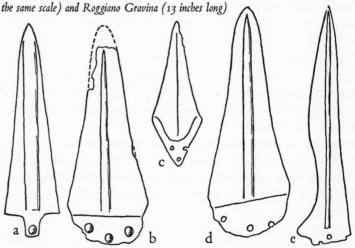

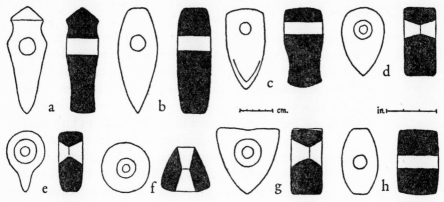

Fig. 24. Copper Age axe-hammers of various forms. Sporadic over Central Italy, now in the Perugia Museum

Rock-cut chamber tombs like this rarely contain a sole interment. Where, as at Casamari near Frosinone, a tomb holds the remains of at least eight skeletons (one, incidentally, with two unhealed trepanations in its skull) it seems most unlikely that death came to them all at the same time. The tomb was barely large enough to hold eight human bodies before they had been reduced to bare skeletons. In fact, in such multiple burials, often only the latest skeleton is found intact, the rest having been swept to the back to make room for it. The dead were believed to retain their personality and power only as long as the flesh remained on their bones. A body in the tomb at Sgurgola even had red ochre smeared on its face, traces having been left on the bones as the flesh disappeared. No such simple remedy can restore the appearance of blood and life to bare bones: the spirit has fled. These, then, are examples of collective burials, family vaults rather than individual tombs, reopened on a number of separate occasions to receive successive interments.

Fig. 18

Among the Rinaldone material, the objects of metal are the most obvious innovations. Axes are of the simplest flat type, but three of the Tuscan tombs had between them five axes

Fig. 42

Fig. 31

with distinct flanges hammered up on their sides to assist in their hafting. These show more advanced working and so are perhaps of a rather later date. Awls, small and of square section, are quite common. The daggers are small also, usually somewhat ogival in form and strengthened by means of either a lozenge-shaped section or a fairly broad low midrib. At the butt end they are either round with a straight top to the hilt-plate or deep triangular with a concave one. Three rivets attached each blade to its haft.

One weapon from Pomarance is slightly asymmetric, which could be dismissed as the result of corrosion if the straight edge of the hilt-plate were not so obviously skew to the axis of the weapon. This makes it look very like a halberd, in which the blade is mounted roughly at right angles to the haft. The only other certain ones from the Rinaldone area are stray finds from Tivoli and 'Etruria'. Part of a broad broken blade from Rinaldone was single-edged and might have come from another halberd, and any of the round-heeled daggers could have been hafted in this manner.

The finest halberd from Italy is undoubtedly that from a tomb at Roggiano Gravina, northern Calabria. It is a 13-inch blade with one edge nearly straight, the other markedly sinuous, and an asymmetric butt. It was found associated with a completely flat tanged copper dagger of primitive shape and two characteristic pressure-flaked flint daggers.

The best known evidence for Italian halberds comes from rock engravings on Monte Bego, in Liguria near the French border. Some 40,000 figures are recorded, those of men and cattle predominating. They are sometimes grouped into charming little ploughing scenes. Amongst the weapons shown, halberds are clearly portrayed, providing the only dating evidence. If we are correct in thinking the halberd to be a West European form of the Copper or Early Bronze Age, these drawings suggest the route by which it entered the peninsula.

The distribution of the metal objects is of interest. The Tuscan tombs are comparatively rich in metal, with a total to date
of 44 pieces. The Fiora area, with more tombs, produced only
27. South and east of these only three have been found in the
Rinaldone area, a dagger with the ochred skeleton at Sgurgola
and two axes. Quite apart from the metal analyses, this is conclusive evidence that as early as this the metal resources of the
Colline Metallifere and Monte Amiata were known and exploited. Although the copper at Monte Bradoni is thought to
be Central European, objects from Ponte San Pietro were of
copper so pure that is was probably native metal, needing no
smelting and local like the antimony.

Equally significant is the distribution of the flint daggers.
They are very similar in outline to the copper ones and virtually
confined to those areas where copper was scarce. They represent
in fact a substitute made by skilled flint workers of the desirable
copper weapons they could not afford. Several fine blades, as
from Osimo, even have the rivet holes worked as notches on
either side of the heel. Whereas those from Latium and the
Marche are usually flaked from both faces, the Campanian ones
often have the main flake surface left on the under side, giving
them a triangular section. Some of these daggers were apparently deliberately broken before being placed in the tomb so
that their 'spirit-substance' could accompany the dead. However, one cannot exclude the cynical possibility that an already
broken and 'dead' weapon might be regarded as adequate
for a dead man whereas it was clearly of no further use to the
living.

Plate 38

Fig. 20

Even commoner than the daggers are the arrowheads. They
vary slightly in size and proportions but are nearly all basically
an isosceles triangle with a short central tang. The barbs too
are short and do not turn back. They occur in nearly every
burial, often in large numbers. The Tomb of the Widow had
15, one of the Rinaldone tombs 29.

Plates 37, 39

cf. *Fig. 24*
Plate 37

Another weapon of war was the ground stone battle-axe or axe-hammer. Though the technique employed was completely different, they are equally finely made, ranging from elaborate forms like that described from the Tomb of the Widow down to simple spherical maces. Cylindrically and biconically per-forated shaft-holes are equally common. Only a drawing can do justice to their variety. They are commonest across Central Italy, no less than ten coming from the nine tombs of Rinaldone itself, and have frequently turned up sporadically, probably from disturbed tombs. The Perugia Museum contains a score or so collected from Umbria and neighbouring regions. This weapon achieved wide popularity, and doubtless considerable respect, throughout Europe during the Copper Age, and symbolises clearly the warlike nature of the period.

Finds from Pianosa and two tombs of the Rinaldone cemetery show that the Neolithic type of polished axe, without shaft-hole, had not yet gone completely out of use. Four tombs, all from the Tusco-Latian group, yielded stone hones like that of the Widow's husband.

Besides tools and weapons, the dead were nearly always given pottery vessels, presumably containing their last earthly meal. Even where they do not survive from early excavations and accidental finds, the reports often mention potsherds which were 'dispersed' or 'crumbled at the touch', as befell only too much pottery in the early days of archaeology.

Plate 37

The characteristic shape is the *bottiglia* described on page 73, for which there is no convenient English name. Decoration is limited to occasional ribs or studs across the shoulder, especial-ly on the Fiora sites. A straight-walled dish is also common, sometimes carinated near the lip. It is without handles and when made in the same fine dark-polished ware as the *bottiglia* looks very like the Neolithic ones in the Lagozza Ware. Coars-er examples with a row of knobs near the rim are closer to Grotta all'Onda forms, but both are so simple that these relationships cannot be insisted upon. The pattern burnish on the Widow's dish is unique in Italy, though the technique is widespread in the eastern Aegean area. A less common shape is a cup with a straight neck on a low curved body, bearing a fairly high strap handle. There are closely similar examples in the Gaudo Culture, to be dealt with next, from which they are likely to have been derived. Like one from the Casamari tomb, they have been found only towards the southern edge of the Rinaldone area. A lid from Garavicchio on the Fiora is even more Gaudo-like, bearing further witness to contacts between the two groups.

Plate 40

Plate 41

In the absence of domestic sites, it is very hard to draw a convincing picture of these people in life. The characteristic which emerges most clearly is that they were warriors. The time and trouble expended on the flint daggers and stone battle-axes is proof of this. By implication, they may have placed more reliance on stock breeding than agriculture, but of this only the missing settlements can give the evidence. The bone of a horse, with those of other domestic animals, was found at Cantalupo Mandela near Tivoli, but as the tomb had been disturbed it cannot be regarded as conclusive evidence of the horse's introduction as early as this. The copper artifacts, particularly their concentration around the ores of southern Tuscany, witness the rise of a local metal industry. At this early stage it may have been only a household craft, though hoards show that it was in the hands of specialist craftsmen at a very early date in the Bronze Age. Trade occurred but is curiously less obvious in the copper objects than in the stone battle-axes and maces. Petrological examination to determine the sources of supply of these would undoubtedly give important results.

The Rinaldone Culture is closely linked with similar developments on the continent. The copper tools and daggers, even more the halberds and battle-axes, all bear witness to this. The round-headed skulls, over a third of those studied, are conclusive of new immigration. The impression is of warrior bands spilling into the peninsula from the north, conquering new homes for themselves which, however, they had to fight to keep.

There is one flaw in this argument, the rock-cut tombs. These, and the collective burial rite which lies behind them, are not Central European but Mediterranean. They had been adopted in Sicily, presumably from the east, about 3000 BC and in Malta by 2700, according to recent radiocarbon dates from the latter. From the northern connections of their contents, their appearance in the Rinaldone Culture cannot be much before 2000 BC. The only radiocarbon reading there, from Luni, gave the closely agreeing figure of 1850 ± 80 BC. So in this respect at least the Rinaldone Culture is of mixed ancestry. It is as well to remember that two thirds of the skulls were long-headed and indistinguishable from ones of Neolithic date. The polish-ed stone axes imply continuity and the pottery too is best ex-plained as of local derivation. The pattern-burnished dish is the only piece which must be foreign, and that is certainly of eastern origin. Perhaps the Mediterranean elements had already penetrated the peninsula during the Final Neolithic. When the bands of warriors introduced the Copper Age from the north, the wives they probably took from the native peoples they con-quered retained their earlier pottery and burial rites, which they persuaded their new husbands to accept.

GAUDO

Beyond the Rinaldone territory, in what is now Campania, flourished the third of these Italian Copper Age cultures, that of Gaudo. The type site is a cemetery of chambered tombs lying just outside the north gate of the ancient Greek city of Paestum, Salerno province. It was discovered when bulldozers levelling the area in 1943 for a military airfield broke through the rock of their roofs. Since then a second rich cemetery has been found at Mirabella Eclano, ten miles south of Ariano. Three poor and isolated burials in the province of Naples, one

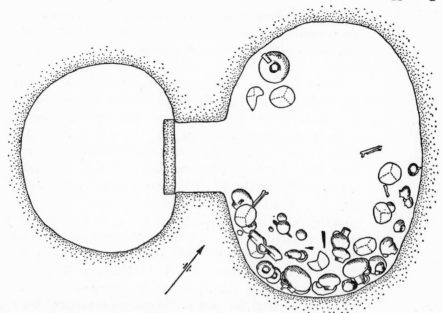

Fig. 25. Tomb in the Gaudo cemetery, Paestum. (After Brinson)

within the city, clearly belong to the same group. It is again a culture known only from its tombs, and our understanding of it suffers accordingly.

These tombs are kidney-shaped and, being cut in level rock, are approached by a vertical entrance shaft. Their orientation is anything but uniform. The Gaudo cemetery was divided by shallow ditches into three areas and there was some evidence that these were successive in time, the tombs towards the south being progressively later. There were even more interments to each tomb than in Rinaldone ones, the number ranging from two to twenty-five. Articulated skeletons were found crouched around the walls accompanied by their pots and weapons. Earlier occupants had been relegated to a disorderly pile at the back while the central space was left clear.

Fig. 25

Grave goods were abundant, particularly the pottery. For example, the first tomb scientifically dug, by the British Army's Mobile Archaeological Unit, held 25 skeletons, 32 pots and seven flint daggers. Metal, however, was extremely scarce. From Gaudo itself there were only two dagger blades, both of rather unusual type. One of the Mirabella tombs yielded a bronze axe but of so advanced a form that it must be a subsequent insertion in the Final Bronze or Iron Age.

The rarity of copper again explains the commonness of the flintwork. The magnificent pressure-flaked flint daggers were individually indistinguishable from Rinaldone ones, and com-paratively much more numerous. There were the same barbed and tanged arrowheads and a few geometric flints which might have served as tranchet arrowheads, with a slashing edge rather than a point. No ground stone tools or weapons appeared.

It is in the wealth, variety and downright oddity of its pottery that Gaudo excels. The most characteristic vessel superficially resembles a Rinaldone *bottiglia,* a squat globular jar with a straight in-sloping collar-neck. The only real difference in sim-ple examples is the handle, a single broad ribbon connecting the base of the neck with the wide shoulder. However, the great majority are distinguished not only from Rinaldone but from all other vessels by the fact that in horizontal section the body approaches a square or triangular form with rounded corners. To call them *askoi* as is usually done is misleading as the name implies a regular tear-drop shape and Aegean or Anatolian connections almost automatically. What seems to have happened is that the potter moved the neck of a *bottiglia* away from its central position to make more room for the large handle. Once the idea of absolute symmetry had been aban-doned, the vessel could be sensibly designed round the handle rather than round the mouth. Until the much later introduc-tion of the potter's wheel, which imposes a circular form on its products, there was no reason why a circle or oval (and ovals

Fig. 20

Plates 40–42

Plate 41

already occurred at Rinaldone) should be preferred to a square
or a triangle. The layout of the Gaudo cemetery gives some
support to this development since it is the most southerly and
so the latest of its tombs which contained the strangest vessels.
The ware is medium to fine and polished, dark and variable
in colour like most of the Copper Age wares. Finger-impressed
cordons sometimes mark the foot of the neck or the sides of the
handle, or more frequently diverge from the root of the latter.
Lightly grooved lines and occasionally dots are also employed.

Three variants of the *bottiglia,* all of smaller size, are a deeper
proportioned simple jug, a wider and longer necked cup with
a large handle (the form which has been noticed straying into
the Rinaldone area) and a curious double vessel. This last comprises two *bottiglia* forms of ampler proportions attached at their
widest girth and joined by a single handle springing from lip
to lip. A decorative knob standing under the loop of the handle
provides the only ornamentation. A truncated conical lid designed to cover the asymmetric jar is frequently decorated, almost invariably with simple geometric designs worked in deeply
jabbed dots. Whereas the grooves occasionally have hints of
Piano Conte or Capo Graziano, the Copper and Early Bronze
Age cultures of Lipari, these dots immediately suggest Conelle-
Ortucchio and the other side of the peninsula.

It is one of these lids which, in the absence of known village
sites, gives the only evidence of the dwellings of the period.
Though its shape may be largely dictated by its function, it
suggests a hut with a low conical roof projecting at the eaves.
A doorway is clearly indicated by the decoration, which also
represents a light construction of wattle, daub and thatch rather
than masonry or mud brick.

When the skeletons were examined, less than a quarter of
the skulls were found to be long-headed. They had other distinctive features such as a low vault, pronounced brow-ridges
and general ruggedness, all of which serve to emphasise the

Plate 37

Plate 42
Plate 40

Plate 41

difference between them and the skulls studied from Neo⁄lithic contexts. The average height of the skeletons was 5 feet 3 inches.

The Gaudo cemetery has been frequently quoted as an exam⁄ple of a sea⁄borne colony from the East Mediterranean, as shown by its position, its *askoi* and its chamber tombs. The discovery of the Mirabella cemetery so far from the coast weakens the first argument; the so⁄called *askoi* are almost certainly an aber⁄rant local development; and similar tombs had been in use for several centuries in the islands to the south. Noticeably lacking are the northern elements like copper weapons and battle⁄axes. In fact, this looks very like the native element postulated in the Rinaldone Culture. In particular, the more open forms of the *bottiglia* shown by the handled and double cups suggest close links with, perhaps direct descent from, the Neolithic *vaso a tocco* tradition. By this interpretation, the round⁄headed skulls remain unaccounted for. If northern, why do no other northern features appear in the material remains? If southern or local, why are they round? If neither, where have they come from? The same problem will reappear in the next section and is best left for discussion then.

Fig. 12

CELLINO

One other area of rock⁄cut tombs is known in the peninsula, Apulia south⁄east of the Ofanto River, with Cellino San Marco between Brindisi and Lecce a good type site. The tombs them⁄selves generally resemble those already described. Cellino differ⁄ed in having three chambers opening from a single shaft, and Altamura, 13 miles north of Matera, in having a sloping ramp or *dromos* in place of the usual vertical shaft. There is also a rock⁄cut tomb at Gioia del Colle south of Bari, an unpublished group at San Vito dei Normanni west of Brindisi, and one found at Vanze south⁄east of Lecce when an Iron Age cairn overlying it was excavated. Although Gioia had only a single interment, Altamura contained the remains of at least ten skele⁄tons and Cellino no less than 77.

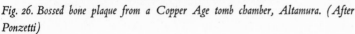

Fig. 26. Bossed bone plaque from a Copper Age tomb chamber, Altamura. (After Ponzetti)

In addition, an ossuary pit at Crispiano near Taranto produced similar material, as did a natural cave used for burials
at Santa Maria al Bagno south-west of Lecce. Related pottery
from Andria at the northern end of Bari province and one jar
from the Gargano must have come from tombs, since pots are
so rarely found complete anywhere else. Conversely, a few
empty tomb chambers probably of this period have been recorded. *Fig. 39*

Only three small and indeterminate scraps of copper were
found, two at Cellino, one at Gioia. On the other hand, Cellino yielded a wide range of stonework: scrapers, knives, blades
and two barbed and tanged arrowheads in flint, together with
two polished axes and four miniature copies serving as amulets.
From Gioia came a fine broad flint dagger, and a curiously
shaped one, rather like a large single-barbed arrowhead, was
found sporadic at Diso near the tip of the Salento.

One of the most interesting finds was an excellent example
of a bossed bone plaque from the Altamura tomb, the only
one yet to come to light in mainland Italy. It is a strip of bone *Fig. 26*
3½ inches long with a strongly curved cross-section, its back
carved into a row of six oval bosses of equal size. A delicate
design is then engraved on the surface round the bosses. The
purpose of these objects is not known, though it has been
suggested that they are highly stylised female figurines. Seven
were found in rock tombs of the Castelluccio cemetery in south-

east Sicily, others on sites of the same culture near by, and one at Tarxien in Malta. One from Lerna in the Peloponnese and several from Troy are of a closely related form.

The pottery is in three different styles, all of which were pres- ent at Cellino itself, though one was very clearly dominant. Elsewhere, oddly, only one style is found at any one site. Since their distributions are completely intermingled, the answer could lie either in the mixing of immigrant strains or in their relative chronology.

The Andria style at least seems to be a local development and the earliest of the three. Its deep bowls vary in form from globular to biconical, often with a single handle. The shoulder is usual- ly decorated with impressions or studs. Though the former are too distant in time to suggest continuity from the old Im- pressed Ware, the latter probably do connect with the Ripoli Studded Ware, perhaps also with a similar ware at Tarxien in Malta. Associated with this style at Gioia was a jug or flask which was certainly foreign, being extraordinarily like exam- ples from Cyprus. Together with the Altamura plaque, it proves connections with the east, whatever the origin of the style as a whole.

Next comes the Cellino style, the standard one at the type site. In this, vases have a long concave neck and a convex body. On the carination which separates the two, a single small handle curves outwards and upwards to an axe edge. The hole through it is small or non-existent. Both vessel and handle are so closely paralleled in the Polada Culture of the Po valley that there must be a link of some kind between the two. Cellino vessels differ in being often decorated. The long neck can bear studs or more often incised cross-hatched bands vaguely recal- ling designs on Beakers (see p. 70 above), or rows of dotted triangles. One has an open dotted design like those of Conelle; others, from Santa Maria and particularly Vanze, have patterns resembling those on the Tarxien Cemetery vessels of Malta.

Plate 43

Plate 44

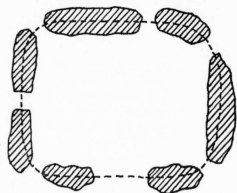

Fig. 27. Sketch plan of the Placa dolmen, Melandugno, Lecce. Cf. Plate 6. (After Jatta)

The typical vessel of the Altamura style is an undecorated bowl with a straight in-sloping shoulder separated by sharp angles from a similar out-sloping neck and a convex body. This has marked resemblances to the Middle Helladic of western Greece, and to finds from Lipari and Malta of the same period. An associated radiocarbon reading of 1930 ± 150 BC was obtained from Malta. The large handle on the Altamura bowl however is quite different, spanning from carination to lip and continuing upwards in a gentle S-curved ribbon. Such handles stand clearly ancestral to the tongue handles of the Apennine Bronze Age. At Crispiano there is more variation of both vessels and handles. One, on a globular jar, has vertical discs added at the top corners and a triangular perforation through the ribbon. On another, the functional strap handle is omitted to leave the ribbon standing alone. It is not easy to say whether this complex is better classified as late Cellino or early Apennine, being so near a mid-point between the Copper and Bronze Age cultures of the area.

Further south in Apulia are found two other classes of monument which may be associated with the Cellino Culture. In a small area south of Lecce around the little town of Otranto, the most easterly in Italy, have been recorded sixteen 'dolmens' of which twelve are still extant. They are all small and of the simplest type, a single capstone of up to 6 feet across supported

Plate 45

Plate 6

Fig. 27

by upright slabs or, a more distinctive feature, pillars built up of several smaller blocks. Sometimes a gap in the wall can be presumed to be a doorway, though there is never any trace of a passage. A common feature is a perforation through the capstone to carry drink offerings down to the dead, implying incidentally that the walls were banked up with a mound which did not completely cover the roof. No trace of such a mound now survives. Some have the rock cut away beneath the capstone to increase the volume of the chamber. Soil erosion and agriculture have between them swept away any deposits, with the result that there are unfortunately no accompanying finds.

Beyond their use of large stones, there is nothing in common between these Otranto dolmens and the megalithic tombs of Taranto and Bari provinces, so the known date of the latter, Final Bronze to Iron Age, cannot be used in evidence. There are no other dolmens geographically nearer then those of Malta, with which the typological links are very close. All the features mentioned can be paralleled except the built pillars. The Maltese dolmens are very nearly as bare of finds, but one yielded a small jar and other sherds of the Tarxien Cemetery Culture, Malta's Early Bronze Age. This has already been mentioned as providing parallels for the dotted sherds of Vanze and Santa Maria al Bagno. The Maltese bossed bone plaque was not from a well-dated level; it could have been from either the cemetery or the preceding temple at Tarxien. The studding on vessels from Cellino and Andria is a common Tarxien technique. Although no link is in itself conclusive, the four together carry some weight as argument for a connection between the two areas. They further argue indirectly in favour of identifying the dolmens with the Cellino Culture, and more specifically with its later Altamura phase.

But linking the two groups of dolmens does not answer the question of the origin of either, the Maltese ones being as foreign there as the Otranto ones are in Italy. Some of the Sardinian dolmens share certain features with these two groups and support a connection with the wide province of megalithic architecture in Western Europe. Proof or disproof of this can come only from the discovery of associated material, pottery or charcoal for radiocarbon dating.

Standing stones or 'menhirs' are found in the same region as the dolmens and rather less commonly elsewhere in the Salento. From their size and distribution, they were probably erected by the same people. 'Menhirs' are stone pillars usually set up singly Plate 9 and apparently without associated deposits, which makes their purpose even more difficult to discover than their date. They may commemorate events or people, or mark religious, political or commercial meeting places. Such abstract concepts have to leave a clearer material record than this before there can be any chance of interpreting them correctly. The problem recurs in acuter form with the Italian statue-menhirs, discussed on p. 98 below. The Salentine menhirs are 10 feet or more high, slim pillars of carefully squared stone. Many have been carved in recent centuries into crosses to exorcise any surviving taint of paganism.

The problem of the origins of the Cellino Culture is even more acute than are those of Gaudo and Rinaldone, since we have to explain traits coming from all four points of the compass. From the north must have come the Cellino style of pottery. From the east we have the Altamura style, the rock-cut tombs generally, and more conclusively the bone plaque and Cypriot flask. From the south are the Sicilian and Maltese connections. A western strain is implied by the dolmens. Finally a local element is represented by the Andria style and the flint and polished stone-work. One fact which emerges clearly from the confusion is that the Italian Copper Age was a period of flux, not to say turmoil, of which the details cannot emerge without much further research.

Can anything further be said of the round-headed skulls here? Evidence from Malta is useful and, in view of the other connections with Apulia, relevant. Its Tarxien Cemetery Culture marks a complete break with the past and indicates an immigration of people from western Greece. No single northern element can be demonstrated. Yet of the few skulls recovered (the normal burial rite was by cremation, as it may have been in the Otranto dolmens) all were round. They also can have come only from western Greece, where the round-headed Alpine race spreads down through the Balkans to the shores of the Mediterranean. Was this people responsible also for the oriental infiltration of Cellino, Gaudo and indeed all Southern Italy in the obscure period between the Neolithic and the Copper Age, bringing with them the rite of collective burial in the rock-cut chambered tomb?

OTHER
GROUPS

By contrast, the other Copper Age cultures of Italy are known only from their settlements; if they also buried their dead in rock-cut tombs, such tombs have not yet come to light. Any comparison between these cultures and those already described is in consequence difficult. For example it is conceivable, though not likely, that Rinaldone and Conelle might pair off as the funerary and domestic aspects of a single culture, and similarly Gaudo and Piano Conte. Deductions must be drawn with caution since discovery of the missing sites, burials and settlements, as the case may be, could upset any conclusions drawn from the inadequate evidence we now have.

The Piano Conte Culture has even stronger links outside the peninsula, though its ultimate origin is as debatable as that of any yet considered. It was first found and is still best known from sites on Lipari, particularly that after which it was named. Until recently it had been found on the mainland, only as stray

Plate 46
Fig. 8

vessels and sherds, at Capri and Ostuni. Now this ware has been discovered in much greater quantity at Paestum, at Praia and in a cave at Morano, 20 miles inland from the last. The marked coastal distribution suggests that sea-borne trade must have played an important part in this people's economy and spread. Traces of it on an inland site like Ariano qualify but do not contradict this statement since Ariano stands on an important trade route across the peninsula. Here was found evidence for the nature of the trade also, in the shape of flakes of obsidian.

Despite the appearance of copper, metal was still far too scarce to oust stone as the raw material of tools and weapons. On the contrary, the flint daggers show that the competition of the smiths encouraged the flint-workers to greater heights of craftsmanship than ever before. In consequence, the demand for obsidian, which had been widely traded from Lipari since Neolithic times, continued unabated. Indeed, a new source was found and exploited on Palmarola in the Pontine Islands but, since its obsidian occurs only as small pebbles, it never became a serious challenge to Lipari. It was doubtless in company with obsidian that the Piano Conte vessels were carried so widely by the traders of Lipari.

It is its decoration which makes this ware immediately obvious in even the smallest sherds. Open dishes and deeper cups and vases all have horizontal grooves so closely spaced and moulded into each other that they form a smoothly corrugated surface. The broad and fairly deep grooves on the fine bowl from the Grotta Ostuni are probably a later and more extreme development of the same idea. Shallower and more widely spaced groovings occur on some vessels, falling into simple patterns such as hatched triangles or chevrons. These suggest an eastern origin for the corrugated decoration, perhaps for the ware as a whole. In the eastern Aegean and western Anatolia, the pattern-burnished and grooved traditions of pot decoration flourished in the Late Neolithic and Copper Age. However, it should be mentioned that an ancestry in the family of Western Neolithic pottery styles has also been suggested for Piano Conte

Plate 46

Central and Southern Italy

Ware. This would place it in a cousinly relationship to Lagozza, which in turn derives from southern France.

Whereas the influence of Piano Conte was due to the obsidian trade, the importance of the Gargano lay in its flint. This region is one of the best explored, yet at the same time one of the least understood, in Italy. The Neolithic cultures seem to have penetrated it little, despite the wealth of the Grotta Scaloria, Coppa Nevigata and the Tavoliere sites along its southern edge. The rugged and forested nature of the country was enough to discourage settlement. A considerable part of it is still wooded, the largest remaining tracts of woodland in the country, aptly known as the Foresta d'Umbra (the Forest of Shadow). Most of the material known probably falls within the Copper Age, with survival into much later periods a strong possibility, as in the closely comparable backwater of the Alpi Apuane.

In stonework the distinctive tool is a coarsely flaked flint axe of the so-called Campignian type. This is slightly more than a convenient term for any flaked axe so rough that it cannot be classified elsewhere since its cutting edge is sharpened by detaching a 'tranchet' flake from the side to intersect the shaping flakes. There is still no reason to suppose any direct connection with the Campignian of France, and similar tools from the Monte Lessini near Verona north of the Po may be equally unrelated. The name of Gargano axes would be more appropriate for this South Italian group.

Fig. 28
'Campignian' flint
axe from Macchia
a Mare, Gargano.
(After Battaglia)

These axes occur sporadically throughout at least the Adriatic side of the peninsula and become common on village sites around the Lake of Lesina and elsewhere through the Gargano. At Tagliacantone near Peschici, sites have been identified where the flint was mined and then flaked into axes in enormous numbers. The quantity of waste flakes on the working floors shows that this must represent a specialised industry, producing for more than local requirements. On the settlement sites many of the flakes were used as simple tools without further working.

Dating is difficult; the tools are so simple as to be deceptively archaic looking, and the working floors themselves yield nothing but flint waste. Even on the few settlement sites known, pottery is scarce and usually of very poor quality, hardly more distinctive than the axes and flakes. Some sherds of a rather finer scratch-decorated ware have been found, particularly at the site of Macchia a Mare. For the rest, these people must have been relying upon vessels made of organic materials, leather or wood, which have not survived for study. It is inconceivable that they had no containers of any kind. The Macchia a Mare sherds show some similarities to material from the Grotta dei Piccioni, Bolognano, which was stratified between Final Neolithic and Bronze Age. Elsewhere the Gargano axes are found in similar Copper Age contexts.

At Bolognano the commonest designs in the fine scratched ware were double zigzags round the lip and vertical feather patterns, particularly inside open dishes. The vessel shapes and ornamentation are both best explained as local developments from the Lagozza Ware which had preceded it here in the Final Neolithic. Associated with it was a coarse smeary ware occasionally bearing interrupted cordons; this, again, derives from the local Neolithic, the coarse cordoned Grotta all'Onda Ware. Closely similar material from Macchia a Mare on one side and the Grotta La Punta in the Fucino on the other sug-   *Fig. 29*
gests that when further sites in this part of Italy are discovered and explored it may prove possible to define another cultural group here parallel to that of Conelle-Ortucchio higher up the Adriatic coast.

At Ariano the continuity with late Lagozza Ware was even   *Plate 4*
more marked. A Neolithic date for this material would never have been doubted but for the associated finds: occasional Rinaldone, Gaudo, Piano Conte and Conelle sherds, various finely worked barbed and tanged, hollow-based, leaf-shaped   *Fig. 20*
and chisel-ended arrowheads and, particularly, a copper awl.

93

This last underlines both the Copper Age date of the deposit and at the same time the extreme poverty of metal away from the centres of production in Tuscany. Although culturally retarded, the inhabitants of Ariano were not completely cut off from the world. As well as the identifiable imports already listed, obsidian from both Lipari and Palmarola was reaching them in some quantity. The trade route from Campania to Apulia which passes the site was obviously still active.

At Ripoli, too, there is no appreciable change in the pottery, but the very number and variety of the arrowheads suggest a date some time later than their first appearance in the Final Neolithic. In particular, a variety with tang and single barb found only on this site is likely to have been a rather later development. The history of this important settlement may become clearer when recent additional excavations are published.

A further example of Neolithic survival is provided by the cave sites in the Alpi Apuane. The Grotta all'Onda Ware continued unaltered, now associated with a Remedello dagger and barbed and tanged arrowheads (Vecchiano), a spherical macehead (Grotta all'Onda itself), three rectangular lumps of shell and a steatite button, all with V-perforations (the Tecchia at Equi and the Tana di Maggiano). Although the Copper Age was a period of major upheaval over much of the peninsula, in corners like these the way of life of the Neolithic farmers continued with little change.

More puzzling are a few sites such as Asciano near the southern end of the Alpi Apuane, the Grotta Ostuni and Sant'Angelo di Cassano. Each has produced material of this period which cannot yet be related to that from elsewhere. The evidence for the cultural fragmentation of the peninsula in the Copper Age is doubtless far from complete. With the spread of unsettled conditions, each region would have tended to develop, or stagnate, in its own way. As further research is carried out, other cultural groups will be defined and, it is hop-

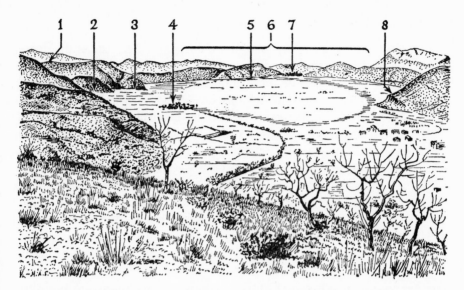

Fig. 29. View of the Fucino from the south-east. 1. Collelongo (Apennine village in side valley) 2. Grotta Ortucchio (Upper Palaeolithic and Mesolithic) 3. Grotte La Punta and Maritza (Palaeolithic to Final Bronze Age) 4. Ortucchio (Copper and Bronze Age open sites, Final Bronze Age urns) 5. Grotta di Ciccio Felice (Upper Palaeolithic) 6. The original lake 7. Avezzano 8. Grotta Clemente Tronci (Upper Palaeolithic)

ed, related to the story taking shape from those already known. It is worth recalling that only twenty years ago Rinaldone was the only culture of the period identified in the peninsula.

Two closely related sites in the Abruzzi and the Marche we have left until last partly because they have been so recently discovered, partly because they sum up so well the problems of the period, the interplay of local development and intrusive influence.

The open village site of Ortucchio stood within a mile or two of La Punta on the shore of what until less than a hundred years ago was the lake of the Fucino. Not surprisingly the excavations revealed more evidence for fishing than for corn growing, for hunting and fowling than for stock raising. A

Fig. 29

95

frequent find for example was a terracotta cylinder too long and heavy to be a bead, too short and narrow to be a water-pipe, so almost certainly a weight for a fishing net. Barbed and tanged arrowheads here were doubtless mainly for hunting and fowling. There were also numerous more simply retouched blades. The villagers were not, however, only hunters and fishers. Amongst their refuse were also sickle flints and domestic animal bones. Spindle whorls and loom weights also imply farming, though no actual cloth survived to show whether vegetable (flax) or animal (wool) fibres were spun and woven.

Conelle di Arcevia is very different, a fortified site of great wealth and interest. The small hill town of Arcevia, 27 miles west of Ancona, overlooks a gravel-floored valley into which the streams have cut their beds deeply. The neck of the low promontory of Conelle between the main stream and one of its larger tributaries was severed by a great artificial ditch over 10 feet deep following a gently sinuous course. Though the excavations under S. M. Puglisi found few traces of the village within these impressive defences, a large amount of domestic rubbish had been incorporated in the silt and tumble from the sides of the ditch, which had in this manner gradually filled until no sign of it remained on the surface.

Plate 10

Here farming was more obviously the basis of the economy. Fishing can have played only a minor part, as the stream below the site is small; yet a net-sinker of the Ortucchio type was included in the finds. Barbed and tanged arrowheads were extremely common, the tang longer and the head broader than is usual. They were further distinguished by the use of an attractive brownish pink opaque flint. Deer bones and antlers suggest one use for these arrows; flint daggers, axe-hammers and the great ditch imply a second and more pressing one. The group of Rinaldone burials around Osimo, some 20 miles east of Conelle, bears witness to an incursion of warrior bands from Umbria, armed with daggers and battle-axes. The local popu-

Fig. 20d

lace, having no mountain barriers to rely on as their relatives at Ortucchio had, were forced to fight to maintain their independence. And to fight successfully they were obliged to adopt the weapons of their enemies.

That they were a local people and not themselves immigrant warriors is shown by their pottery. The coarse ware is again of Grotta all'Onda type, as shown by its fabric and finger-impressed cordons. The finer ware seems to be another late development of the Lagozza tradition, in some ways resembling the Bolognano Ware mentioned above. The open dishes with simple handles, mere lugs or lip projections, or with no handles at all, have altered little. More interesting are baggy ovoid jugs with a sloping mouth and a simple vertical handle. The finest example has a curious spout through the wall, which renders the lip useless.

Plate 47

The major innovation in this ware, balancing some deterioration in its fabric and finish, is its band ornament produced by rows of deeply jabbed dots. It is confined to the jugs and jars, on which the bands form simple rectilinear designs. This decoration occurs also, if rather more rarely, at Ortucchio and a typical jug, with the extra spout, was recovered from Belverde di Cetona. The technique of dotting is in itself so simple that caution must be exercised in basing connections on it alone. On the other hand it seems more than coincidence that in the same chronological horizon it appears on some Cellino vessels, on Gaudo lids, on sherds from Ariano and on pots from a tomb at Drauto on Salina, the neighbouring island to Lipari. The possibility of this ware being ancestral to some of that of the Apennine Bronze Age is mentioned on page 120.

Plate 11

The evidence for far-reaching connections offered by the dotted decoration is in itself far from conclusive but it is supported by other finds. Even away from the long-established obsidian routes of the south and the lines of warrior penetration in the north, there was a slow percolation of ideas through the peninsula. Incised zigzags across the base of the Belverde jug are extraordinarily like examples in the same position on bowls of the Capo Graziano phase, which succeeded Piano Conte on Lipari. A typical Gargano axe was found at Conelle. From the same site came a single small fragment of copper related by its analysis to Remedello metal and derived ultimately from Central Europe.

The most remarkable example of cultural diffusion is provided by what are usually referred to as 'statuemenhirs'. As their name is meant to imply, they are standing stone slabs or oval pillars carved with features giving them some semblance of human form: a face, breasts, a necklace, an axe or dagger. They were first recognised in France, where good examples have been found built into megalithic tombs, as at Collorgues and TretsOrgon in Provence, or carved upon rockcut chamber tombs, as in the Paris Basin. Many are, however, unassociated, like the particularly fine example at Saint Sernin in the Aveyron. Another group from Corsica, named after the site of Filitosa, has a rather different and plainer appearance.

Fig. 30 Four groups occur in Italy, all unassociated. Six examples have been found at Lagundo, Merano, near the Austrian and Swiss borders. Three more came to light recently at Castelluccio de' Sauri at the southern edge of the Tavoliere in Apulia. A large number in the valley of the Magra at the extreme northwest corner of Tuscany have been divided into two on stylistic grounds and called after examples at Pontevecchio and Filetto, together being known as the Lunigiana group. The Filetto group can be left out of consideration for the moment, being obviously much later (see p. 166).

The rest are simpler and more like the French ones. Those from Castelluccio have breasts, necklaces and on one fragment a dagger with triangular blade and round pommel. The face and arms are not shown. The Lagundo examples are similar, with daggers much commoner. At Pontevecchio the face is

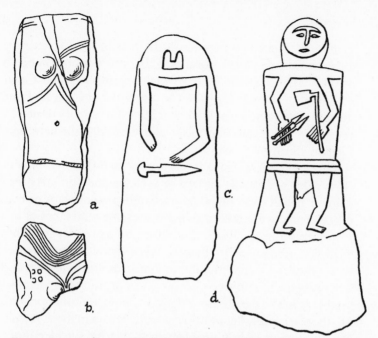

Fig. 30. Statue-menhirs. a and b, Castelluccio de' Sauri (after Acanfora); c, Ponte-vecchio and d, Filetto types, Magra valley (after Formentini)

represented in schematic form and the arms more clearly. Some here are clearly female, with breasts and no weapons; more have only a dagger and could be of either sex. One of these daggers has a strongly marked midrib, like those represented at Lagundo, and can be much better paralleled in actual weapons at Remedello than anywhere else. This, together with the French connections, leads us to suppose a Copper Age context or, at least, origin for all three groups since stylistically they are clearly related.

This leaves two problems outstanding. When found in tombs, as in France, these figures are taken to be representations of the Earth Mother, the divinity who watches over death as

99

well as life. Her necklace and dagger imply that here is the same person, even when standing in the open countryside far from any known burial or dwelling. What then is she doing there? Did men believe that their efforts in setting up these blocks carved with her features would be repaid by her protection of their fields and homes? We could acknowledge defeat in our efforts to understand the plain menhirs of the Salento easily – there were so many possibilities and there was so little to work on. The additional clues offered by the statue-menhirs make them more intriguing but help hardly at all with their interpretation. Guesswork is the only course remaining.

The second problem is why these three groups of statue-menhirs are so widespread in their distribution. They resemble each other and the French examples so closely that there must be an intimate connection between them. How and why, in the troubled times of the Italian Copper Age, did their makers travel the length of the country to leave such convincing, yet baffling, proof of their journey? For this, too, we shall need far more evidence before being able to hazard anything more than unsupported guesses.

CHAPTER V

The Bronze Age

EARLY BRONZE AGE

T HE CHANGE from the Copper to the Bronze Age is primarily an economic, or more strictly a technological, advance. In this sense it can be documented only in that region of
the peninsula where metal was in common use, namely southern   *Fig. 32*
Tuscany. The addition of tin to the copper produces an alloy
with three main advantages: it is harder and so more durable; it
melts at a lower temperature, making working easier; and it is
much less likely to form flaws in the process of casting than is
pure copper. Unfortunately the natural ores of tin are very much
scarcer than those of copper.

The introduction of the new alloy was not the only example
of progress at this time. More efficient forms of axe and dagger   *Fig. 42*
were developed either locally or under stimulus from outside.
Difficulty must have been found in holding the simple flat axe
of the Copper Age firmly in the cleft of its haft. Now the crafts-
man gave the blade a much better grip on the wood by hammering or casting its sides into flanges, which prevented any
up and down movement. And the tendency for the haft to
be split in use was averted by casting the axe blade with a
notch in the butt. A dowel passed through this would both
spread the strain of impact and hold the blade more rigidly.

The daggers were now fashioned with a longer blade and
more graceful outline. At the same time, attention was paid
to their hafting also, the more efficient deeply indented hilt-
plate replacing that with a straight top. Alongside these, a new
form appeared in which the hilt was cast in bronze in one piece
with the blade. A delicate chased decoration on the blade and   Plates 56, 57
sometimes also on the hilt enhanced the pleasing outline to
make these weapons objects of real beauty. They were not, how-

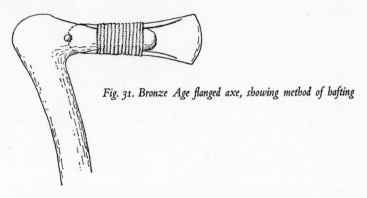

Fig. 31. Bronze Age flanged axe, showing method of hafting

ever, the products of local craftsmen but imports from the metal-working centres of the Únĕtice (Aunjetitz) Culture in Bohemia, brought by traders south to Italy across the Brenner Pass. These two types, axe and dagger, complete the limited range of shapes recorded from the period. An armlet amongst a hoard discovered in 1674 at Noceto near Forlì is likely to be of later date. A wedge and cakes of bronze from hoards near Siena are ingots or pellets of unworked metal.

The fact that these finds are nearly all hoards is itself the third and most important difference, since it illustrates a real economic advance on Copper Age practice. Metal of that period comes solely from tombs; very few burials of the Early and Middle Bronze Age have come to light, and of these at most two have yielded objects of metal. A cist grave found at Parco dei Monaci (Monks' Park) just south of Matera contained a flanged axe, a solid-hilted dagger and the blade of a simple flat dagger. A group of objects from Montemerano near the Fiora River, comprising three flanged axes, two dagger blades and a pellet of metal, was perhaps also a tomb group. Here analysis showed that the axes were of poor bronze and the other objects of copper, illustrating the moment when the addition of tin to the metal was just coming into fashion.

Fig. 9

Fig. 33

Fig. 32. Bronze Age sites and regions

1. The Terremare
2. Bologna (Farneto, Prevosta, etc.)
   See Fig. 59
3. Bismantova (urnfield)
4. Loiano (hoard)
5. Imola (Toscanella Imolese, Monte
   Castellaccio)
6. Noceto, Forlì (hoard)
7. Alpi Apuane
8. Le Galleraie, Siena
9. Grotta dello Scoglietto, Monti
   Uccellini
10. South Tuscan hoards
11. Belverde di Cetona; Casa Carletti
12. Ponte San Pietro
13. Luni, Monte Romano
14. Allumiere (urnfield) and Coste del
    Marano (hoard)
15. Pian Sultano, Santa Severa
16. Gola del Sentino (Pianello urnfield,
    Spineto, Frasassi, etc.) See Fig. 45
17. Santa Paolina, Filottrano
18. Ripatransone (hoard)
19. Grotta Sant'Angelo, Salinello
20. Gran Sasso (Campo Pericoli and
    Grotta a Male, Assergi)
21. Fucino (Collelongo, Grotta La
    Punta, Ortucchio, etc.) See Fig. 29
22. Grotta dei Piccioni, Bolognano
23. Grotta Manaccora, Peschici
24. Coppa Nevigata
25. Bari gallery graves (Bisceglie,
    Albarosa, Giovinazzo, etc.)
26. Terlizzi
27. Bari
28. Taranto (Scoglio del Tonno, Torre
    Castelluccia, etc.) See Fig. 39
29. Matera (Murgia Timone, Timmari
    urnfield, etc.) See Fig. 9
30. Grotta Latronico
31. Grotta Pertosa
32. Albanito, Paestum
33. La Starza, Ariano Irpino
34. Camposauro, Monte Taburno,
    Benevento
35. Castiglione d'Ischia and Vivara. See
    Fig. 52
36. Grotta delle Felci, Capri
37. Lago Ampollino, Cotronei (hoard)
38. Tropea (urnfield)
39. Milazzo (urnfield)
40. Lipari (Citadel, Piazza Monfalcone, etc.)

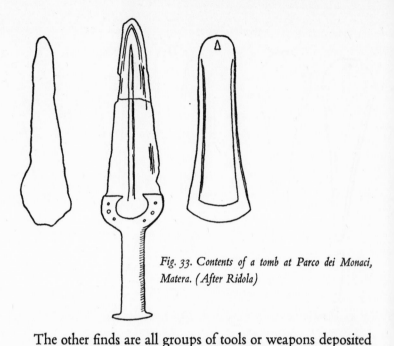

Fig. 33. Contents of a tomb at Parco dei Monaci, Matera. (After Ridola)

The other finds are all groups of tools or weapons deposited in the ground away from either settlements or burials. Various classes of hoard are recognised depending on how they were amassed and why they were buried. To take one example, the twenty-five magnificent and unused daggers of the Ripatran-sone hoard were obviously not needed by an individual for his own defence. For that, one is sufficient, two are possible, three or more an embarrassment. If twenty-five men for some reason buried their weapons together, it is surprising that they should all be new blades, from a distant source. Consequently it is difficult to explain the hoard other than as the stock-in-trade of a travelling merchant, bringing his wares from the far-off manufacturing centres of Bohemia. Doubtless he hid them when some danger threatened, or left in a place of safety all but the few samples he needed to show to potential cus-tomers. What accident prevented his returning to recover the rest of his property we shall never know. That the dangers of

Plates 56, 57

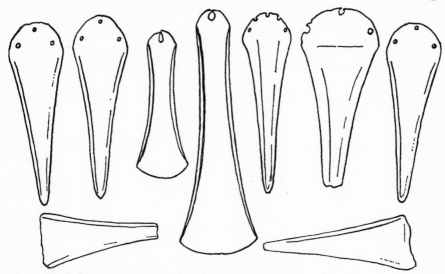

Fig. 34. Hoard of daggers and axes from the Lago Ampollino, Cotronei

such trade, considerable as they must have been, were no barrier is shown by four hoards of these daggers in the peninsula,
and single ones as far south as the Matera tomb just mentioned.

In a category of its own is another hoard found recently at
Cotronei, beside Lake Ampollino in the heart of the Calabrian
Sila. It comprised two flanged axes and seven dagger blades.   *Fig. 34*
It has been suggested that these daggers too are Central European, so even further from their place of origin. Their find-
spot by a mountain lake, a place perhaps of some sanctity,
suggests that they might be not a merchant's hoard but a votive
one, of objects offered to a divinity with no intention of reco-
very. Such were many of the magnificent finds from the North
European peat bogs and rivers, and clear examples will be
quoted from the Italian Late Bronze Age.

The other hoards rarely contain anything but flanged axes,
sometimes in surprising numbers. Over forty were found together in each of four hoards: two near Siena, one at Loiano

near Bologna and one, including also solid-hilted daggers, from Noceto. These, again, look like merchants' hoards. Their significance is increased by a study of their distribution. Of the sixteen axe hoards known, ten came to light in the provinces of Siena and Grosseto within 30 miles of Monte Amiata. It is just this area which produced the majority of the Rinaldone metal finds and where the natural deposits of copper lie. The ores of the Colline Metallifere just to the north-west were apparently not exploited until a rather later date. A certain amount of tin must also have been available here, although the ores were probably worked out in antiquity. There can be no doubt that these hoards are the products of a local industry based on local metal.

The implication is that society had developed to a point where specialist industry and trade, possibly both carried out by the same persons, could play their parts in the economy. The hoards themselves suggest that the trade was still a hazardous one. They were left for us to find only because their original owners were prevented from recovering them. The unsettled conditions of the Copper Age seem only gradually to have subsided.

For the sake of continuity, it is worth pursuing the story of the metalwork even though some of these hoards may more properly belong to the Middle Bronze Age. No developments of the axe and dagger, nor introduction of other types, can be traced until trade was opened with the bronze-working culture of the *terremare* (p. 128 below) in the Late Bronze Age. The metals of Monte Amiata were certainly worked throughout this period but they played no part in the developments in Northern Italy and had little effect even on the rest of the peninsula.

In consequence, the story of the Bronze Age outside Tuscany must be pieced together from other evidence, which it must be admitted is very scanty for its opening stages. It is made more difficult by the fact that very little else has been found in the homeland of the hoards. If we knew more about the styles of pottery current there at the time, we might be able to trace their connections in other regions. Only two sites have come to light in the district, Le Galleraie near Siena and the Grotta dello Scoglietto (Cave of the Little Rock) near Grosseto, the latter yielding another trepanned skull. The pottery from these is neither distinctive nor related to the standard Bronze Age ware of the peninsula. Here it looks as if the cultural fragmentation of the Copper Age continued until the Middle Bronze Age, when Tuscany can again be linked with the main story of Italy. Similarly the north Tuscan sites like Asciano and the Alpi Apuane clearly pursued their own courses little altered.

Central Italy from Rome to Ancona supported a very rich cultural development in the Middle Bronze Age, the northern branch of the Apennine Culture. Its antecedents are, however, very obscure. It seems most unlikely that a site like Belverde di Cetona should have been abandoned at the beginning of the Early Bronze Age and reoccupied at the end of it. In the ab- sence of stratified deposits, we can only point to certain material from that site which is probably of this date, leaving a full description of the Apennine Culture until the much better documented Middle and Late Bronze Age. From Belverde have come a number of handles of curious form not found elsewhere in the peninsula but occurring in Liguria and Emi- lia. They consist of a broad rectangular ribbon rising in an S-curve from the shoulder of their vessel and stopping abruptly at a thickened or rolled tip. Many low carinated dishes here have rectilinear designs worked in dotted bands without en- closing lines. Since they can be related to the dotted decoration of the Conelle Ware, they may also go back to the earliest stages of the Bronze Age in this area.

Plate 11

What remains to be found is deposits of this period either in stratified levels or, failing that, in unmixed short-lived sites. We cannot believe that the local antecedents of the rich Apennine Culture can escape detection in Central Italy for much longer.

Plate 4

In Southern Italy we are fortunate in having two sites which meet these requirements. At Ariano, occupation on the gypsum hill of La Starza continued unbroken, the manifest advantages of the site remaining as long as the route across the peninsula which it controlled was still in use. Its abandonment came only when settlements increased in size in the Iron Age to a point where the hill-top could no longer support a flourishing village. Already by the Early Bronze Age the settlement had spread down the northern slope of the hill. Erosion has removed most of the relevant levels from the exposed summit, but they have been preserved on a broad terrace which probably served primarily as a corral for the stock and as a dumping place for refuse from the village above. The only structures revealed here were small hearths, perhaps watch-fires.

Culturally there was no direct evidence on the change from Copper to Bronze. No more metal was found until the Late Bronze Age levels, so to call the intermediate period a Bronze Age at all is somewhat misleading, however convenient. The pottery provides the information we are seeking on the origins of the Apennine Culture to be described in the next section.

During the Copper Age, the inhabitants of La Starza had shared in a late and stagnant version of the Lagozza Culture, the roots of which ran far back into the Neolithic of Northern Italy. As a result of stimulus provided by contact with the bearers of the Cellino Culture to the south-east, the opening of the Bronze Age was marked by renewed development. It was, however, a gradual change. The fabric of the pottery, a dark burnished ware, continued unaltered. The open Lagozza dishes declined steadily in popularity relative to the carinated ones, the necks of which were progressively more emphasised by the potters. To them were added axe and tongue handles of the types already noticed at Altamura and Crispiano in the preceding period, making vessels quite distinct from any previously current. These 'typical' Apennine carinated bowls are so extremely variable that the term is almost meaningless. At the same time to the fine ware was added a coarse cordoned ware for use in the kitchen, derived ultimately from Grotta all' Onda Ware (see p. 58).

An important element of the full Apennine Culture was still noticeably lacking. No decorated sherd was found in these levels. The scratched Lagozza designs had dropped out of favour and nothing had yet been developed by the potters to replace it.

That this is not a local aberration at the one site is proved by the material excavated many years ago from the Pulo di Molfetta. That site had been abandoned in the later Neolithic and was reoccupied briefly in the Early Bronze Age. The circular inward-facing cliff bounding it was riddled with caves, forming a ready-made village. These yielded quantities of pottery exactly like that from the levels at Ariano just described, carinated bowls of a dark burnished ware with axe and tongue handles but no decoration whatsoever.

Plate 2

MIDDLE BRONZE AGE

The Middle Bronze Age in Italy is the great period of the Apennine Culture, so called because it brought cultural unity to the whole of the Apennine peninsula, the local groups forming the patchwork of the Copper Age being gradually assimilated. This cannot be due to military conquest, since there is a marked decrease in evidence for warfare. Comparatively few of the known sites are set in defensive positions and even fewer had artificial defences. Bronze daggers are remarkably scarce and flint daggers and stone battle-axes are unknown. Even flint arrowheads are rarely found.

A more interesting suggestion has been put forward recently by S. M. Puglisi: that the uniformity can be explained in economic terms. At this period stock-breeding appears to have

increased greatly in importance, at first perhaps encouraged by
the unsettled conditions of the Copper Age. Whereas crops
have to be abandoned to the enemy or destroyed, stock can be
driven to a place of safety. The preference for animal husbandry
continued when peace returned.

Many sites of the period are in a type of countryside hardly
likely to appeal to a farmer. It is difficult to see how the inhabit-
Plate 13, *Fig. 45* ants of the caves in the rugged sides of the Gola del Sentino
could have supported themselves by crop-growing. As pastor-
alists they would have had no problem. More conclusive still is
an Apennine Culture site on the Campo Pericoli, a plateau
standing at an altitude of 7000 feet above sea level near the peak
of the Gran Sasso, the highest mountain in the peninsula. Even
sites like the Grotta a Male at Assergi, lower down on the same
mountain, and Camposauro near the peak of Monte Taburno
above Benevento at around 4000 feet would have been under
snow for several months every winter. They can be explained
only as seasonal camps to take advantage of the good mountain
grazing in the summer. In the autumn the flocks and herds
would have been driven down to the valleys and coastal plains
until the spring. This annual ebb and flow still sets the pattern
of life in the mountainous heart of the country, though now it is
the hill villages which are the permanent ones, the shepherds
living in temporary camps while down in the plains.

The mobility of settlement, in particular of opportunities for
the exchange of ideas in the summer camps, would tend to foster
that very cultural unity shown in the material record. Whether
there were more deliberate gatherings comparable to the cattle
fairs of later times, even more productive of cultural exchange,
is unlikely at least until later in the Bronze Age.

Certain curious pottery vessels occurring in various parts of
the peninsula have been ingeniously explained in terms of a
pastoralist economy. They are rare in Copper Age contexts,
become common in the Bronze Age and disappear before its

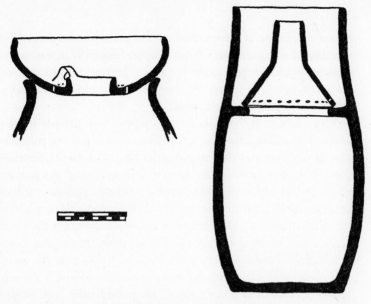

Fig. 35. Apennine Culture milk-boiling vessels; the southern form on the left (from the Grotta Pertosa), the northern on the right (from Belverde)

end. The first of these vessels was known as a *bugia,* or candle-stick, which it resembles in form, until its real function was realised. It consists of a shallow bowl, curved or angular, with a large circular hole through the centre of its base surrounded by a collar. The valley between collar and wall is pierced by a ring of smaller holes and bridged by a single handle. Its pur-pose was to prevent accidents during the slow boiling of milk in some processes of cheese-making. When placed over the mouth of a jar, any boiling milk would rise through the central hole, burst its bubbles of steam with the sudden release of pres-sure in the open air and drain harmlessly back through the smaller holes into the jar below.

This form of bowl is found only in Southern Italy. Its coun-terpart further north was an inverted funnel, usually with a ring of holes near its wider lip. The spout might occasionally have

Fig. 35

a handle attached to it. Except that it had to be used with a special jar, having an internal ledge to support it, it functioned in exactly the same way as the bowl. Funnels of this form were in use into the earlier part of this century in country districts. Other vessels have been interpreted in similar ways though none is so conclusive. Perforated strainers or dipper-sieves would serve admirably for separating curds from whey, but there are other equally likely possibilities. Miniature jars may have been used to store rennet in small quantities for curd-ling milk but, being found in such enormous numbers at the sacred site of the Grotta Pertosa, they are more likely to have themselves been votive offerings. As with the sites, then, some vessels are supporting evidence for a pastoralist economy, many are compatible with it, and some must be explained in other ways.

Even if reduced to second place in the economy, agriculture remained of importance. The inhabitants of sites such as the Grotta delle Felci on Capri, for example, could hardly have been transhuming stock-rearers. Querns of hard stone for grind-ing the grain by hand are known from a number of sites. When bronze became common in the Late Bronze Age, sickles were among the tools produced. Grain itself has survived in the caves of Belverde, preserved by charring. Here were found not only wheat and barley but acorns in large quantities, possibly also used for food after the bitter tannin had been pressed out. The horse bean, *Vicia faba,* was grown, as its larger descendant the

Fig. 36

Plate 60
Plate 11

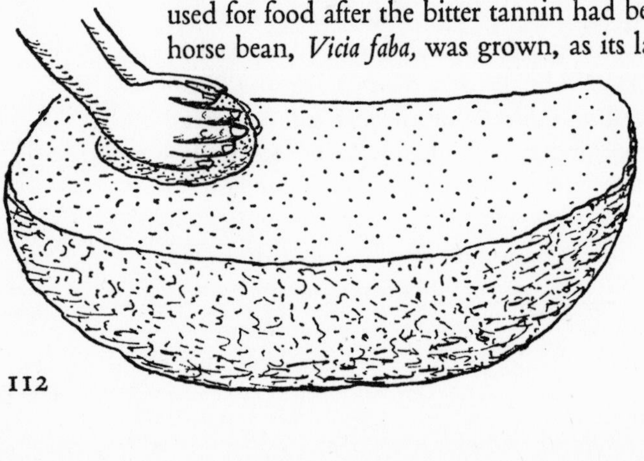

Fig. 36. Stone quern and rubber for grinding corn by hand

broad bean still is; the field pea, *Pisum arvense,* likewise. Other species recorded were the broom-corn millet (*Panicum miliaceum*), cornel and the grape vine. Unfortunately it was not found pos-sible to date the various deposits at Belverde closely. The vine, for example, is not otherwise reliably recorded from Italy before the first millennium and it may well be as late as that here.

Domestic animals are much more easily recognised, identi-fied and even counted from bones surviving in rubbish deposits. The figures obtained from the Bronze Age levels at Ariano can be taken as typical. There, 42% of the animal bones were of sheep or goat, 31% of cow, 19% of pig and 3% of dog. Wild species like the deer and tortoise accounted for the remaining 5%, too few to suggest that hunting figured largely in the eco-nomy. These proportions are remarkably close to those of the livestock kept at the farm on the site today. The only animal missing is the horse, though it had by this time been introduced into Northern Italy.

Plate 4

Whether pastoralists, agriculturalists or both, the Apennine farmers of this period had a very limited material equipment. As already mentioned, their sites have produced hardly any bronze. Perhaps it is unfair to assume from this that they had none, since there is a marked decrease in the use of stone for tools. Some arrowheads of flint continued, together with scrap-ers and knife blades, but even these disappeared in the course of the period. The contrast with the wealth and skill of the immediately preceding flint industry is startling, and the decline seems most easily explained by the new material, bronze, driv-ing the old off the market. Unlike flint, bronze can be readily re-used when worn out and is too valuable to be lightly dis-carded. The only stone artifacts to continue in any quantity were the querns.

Fig. 36

Though flint ceased to be common and bronze did not be-come so until the Late Bronze Age, bone was extensively used for small tools like pins, needles, awls and spatulas. These were most commonly ground from the split cannon-bones of sheep. Wood, leather, basketry and other perishable materials may also have been employed but have left virtually no trace. Some

Plate 51

pottery decoration should be recalled as it appears to copy a chip-carved technique from woodwork.

The impression given so far is of a poor and stagnant culture without a gleam of inspiration, ignoring new skills and often allowing old ones to lapse into oblivion. A glance at the pottery will immediately dispel any such illusion. In some ways it equals the finest of the Neolithic wares, in others it moves with assurance into fields of which its predecessors can scarcely have had an inkling.

There is little to see of this in the coarse kitchen ware, which continues scarcely altered from the earlier periods. It is service-able but not beautiful, even when cordons are applied in an

Plate 55

occasional attempt at decorative treatment. The finer ware gave

Plates 48-53

the potter more chance to show her craft. (Until the potter's wheel turned pot-making from a domestic chore into a special-ised industry, it was nearly always left to the womenfolk, as amongst many primitive peoples today.) The fabric was hand-made and dark in colour. Burnishing improved its appearance by giving it a shiny surface and its ability to hold water by compacting its clay.

There is an extraordinarily wide range of vessel shapes: plat-

Fig. 35

ters, basins, jugs, cups, the milk-boilers already referred to, and, commonest of all, a bowl so varied that there is no word in

Plates 50-53

English general enough to translate the Italian *capeduncola*. The variation lies largely in the length, profile and angle of its prominent neck. Though it usually has a carination, a low body and a small flat base, none of these features is universal. The outside of the neck, more rarely the lip and body also, may be

Plates 50, 51

decorated. An invariable feature is the presence of a single handle, which can be of even more varied shape. This suggests that the bowl probably did duty as a drinking vessel, despite its large size and weight. What beverages were served in it can only be guessed.

The characteristic decoration is of bands made up of dots or ladder bars between parallels, two parallel lines without filling, a broad cut-out line, a false relief zigzag of opposed rows of triangles, or the like. The bands are then formed into simple bold geometric designs. Rectilinear ones are based on triangles, Plates 48–51 chevrons, chequers, lozenges, Greek key patterns, dog-legs, interrupted or continuous meanders, positive or negative, set upright or diagonally. Curvilinear bands are less easy to classify since they include such a wide variety of arcs, S's, loops, spirals, tadpoles and so on. The designs were filled with a white inlay the better to show up against the dark polished pot surface.

Where the Apennine potters really excelled, however, was in the modelling of the handles they gave to their carinated bowls. Two main classes are distinguishable, characteristic of the south and north of the peninsula respectively. The southern one derives from the elongated tongue handle of the Copper Fig. 37 Age. It is basically a more or less rectangular projection from the lip of the vessel, to the back of which a small strap handle may still be attached. This tongue is always saddled and curved outwards towards its tip, the corners of which are then often twisted. It is usually perforated at the centre, possibly for hanging up. At later stages in its development its curves become more pronounced, until the effect is like some abstract piece of sculpture.

The northern handle starts from a different origin altogether, a normal rim-to-carination strap handle given a projection at the top. In this way the thumb round the projection could help Fig. 38 the forefinger through the strap in supporting the weight of the vessel. In one development the projection is enlarged into a knobbed pillar, the *ansa a cilindro-retta*. A more versatile and Fig. 38b consequently more popular handle with the potters employed in place of the simple knob a pair of horns in T- or Y-shaped

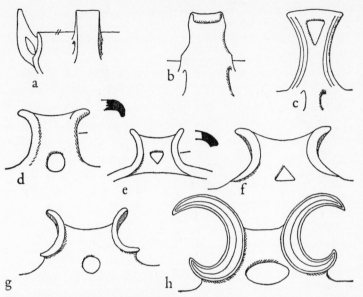

Fig. 37. Apennine tongue handles and developments. From left to right: axe, Bari-axe and tongue and strap handles; typical tongue handle, rim-bevelled and separate bevelled; early Filottrano and Filottrano lobster-claw handles

Plate 54, Fig. 38a

cf. Plate 65
Fig. 38g
Fig. 38e
Fig. 38f
Fig. 38i

form, the *ansa cornuta*. The horns take on various shapes, their suggestion of an animal's head often being emphasised by the addition of a muzzle below them. For variety this cow's head may be replaced by a dog's or even a duck's, and so on. Another series begins with a handle drawn up into a radial crest, leading to elaborate knobbed or perforated projections. And yet another with a transverse crest or axe begins a further series of developments. The potters obviously had a great feeling for, and delight in, shapes. They seem to have been much less hampered than usual by the conservatism of primitive communities, following up freely any ideas a given shape suggested to them.

With a culture so variable in detail, occupying a territory of such size and diversity as the Italian peninsula, it is inevitable that there should be regional variation. To illustrate this, a num-

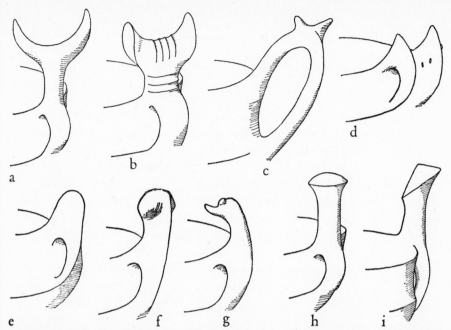

Fig. 38. Apennine elaborate handles. From left to right: top row, horned handles of the Central Italian, Terramara, Trojan and Taranto types; lower row, crested, Nevigata, duck-headed, pillar and spatula-headed handles

ber of the more important sites will be described in some detail. This will have the additional advantage of bringing in other aspects of the Apennine Culture for which evidence may be available from only one or two of the sites.

For example, the Grotta Pertosa and Belverde di Cetona are the only places to give information, albeit scanty, on the religious beliefs of the Apennine folk. Pertosa is a large cave opening in the steep side of the Tanagro valley in southern Campania. From it flowed a sizable stream, to cascade down to the main river below. When it was dammed and piped to produce hydro-electric power, it was found that the cave had been of interest to man from early times. In the Middle Bronze Age it served as a dwelling, as did so many other Italian caves. The advantages of a plentiful running water supply had more than outweighed the disadvantages of a swampy floor, which could be covered with a wooden platform supported on piles to keep the occupants out of the damp. The former view that this timberwork provided evidence for influence from the *terremare* of the Po valley (see p. 128 below) is no longer held. Apart from the remains of the platform and piles preserved by waterlogging, the great quantities of pottery and other domestic refuse found were typical of Apennine sites throughout Campania.

cf. Plate 52
cf. Plates 49, 50 The southern tongue handles were very common and the band decorations were frequent, particularly in their curvilinear form. A flanged axe and awl were the only objects of bronze.

But apparently the stream came to have an importance beyond its mere convenience. Besides the domestic material within the cave, an enormous number of miniature vessels was found, averaging some 2 inches high. A few of these could have been containers for special commodities like perfume (unlikely in a primitive community such as this) or as children's toys. But so large a quantity suggests that they were votive offerings, small cheap copies of domestic jars offered to the divinity of the stream and cave. Outside its entrance was found a rich hoard of metal objects of Late Bronze Age date, also votive in character. The sanctity of the site continued, as is shown by further Greek and Roman offerings, the latest being a coin of Justinian of the seventh century AD. It is interesting to see the worship of the rustic deities of classical times, the nymphs, going back so much earlier.

Belverde is less clearly marked out by nature as a sacred site. A spur from Monte Cetona projects into the hill country of
Plate 11 southern Tuscany, terminating in a cliff of travertine. Below this is a tumble of rocks fallen from the cliffs and now overgrown with evergreen oaks. A hermitage turned into a farm is the only modern dwelling. The Bronze Age finds came mainly from caves and crevices between the rocks. Again, many of them look like votive offerings, particularly the jars of char

red grain (burnt sacrifices) and a surprising quantity of Late Bronze Age metalwork. Some skeletons showed that these crannies also served as a cemetery for the round-headed population. A little lower down the slope were traces of an open hut-village, but better evidence on Apennine Culture dwellings will be described from other sites shortly. On the crest of the cliff can be seen the tumbled remains of a defensive stone wall which has not yet been fully investigated and may be of much later date.

The oddest feature of the site is that many of the larger rocks have their summits carved into artificial shapes. In one, the 'Amphitheatre', rows of what look like seats have been cut round three sides of a rectangular 'stage', more likely for religious or political events than for dramatic ones. The fourth side is open and drops steeply away. In a second example, the 'Observatory', the carvings would be dismissed as the relics of quarrying but for the difficulty of access to the isolated crag which they crown. They are therefore deliberate, though for what purpose one cannot now say. Many other similarly puzzling examples occur on the site and a few are known elsewhere in the district between Siena and Perugia. They serve to emphasise the impossibility of obtaining any clear understanding of the religious beliefs of societies which lack writing.

Plate 12

The material from this site could not be dated stratigraphically. The metalwork is certainly largely of Late Bronze Age types but the pottery must cover the earlier phases also. This is proved by the site of Luni, 50 miles to the south, where identical finds were associated with sherds of Mycenaean pottery and a radiocarbon date in close agreement with them, 1245 ± 80 BC. The importance of the Mycenaean contacts will be examined shortly. The Apennine pottery of this part of Italy differs in many details from that of the south. Tongue handles do not occur and only later do the northern elaborate handles become common. Decoration on bowls and jars is less frequent, usually rectilinear and with designs often closer to those of Conelle in the Copper Age than to the normal Apennine band ornament.

Luni shows a different type of rock carving. Here a plateau of tuff had been cut into by deeply eroding streams. Erosion had subsequently broken through the neck of a promontory between two of these streams, leaving a level cliff-girt site which had attracted settlement from Neolithic times on. In the Bronze Age, defences were felt to be necessary but the village was not large enough to occupy the whole of the hill-top. A line of rectangular trenches 7 feet wide and 5 deep, the longest 140 feet long, was cut across the breadth of the promontory, presumably to separate the village proper from a bailey for the cattle. The outermost trenches in the line open directly on to the cliff edges. The widest causeway between the trenches revealed post-holes, suggesting a wooden entrance gateway.

Apart from fragments of daub, no sign of huts was found within these defences, possibly because they were of too light a construction to leave any permanent mark. A more intriguing possibility is that the inhabitants of the site were actually living in the ditches. It is difficult otherwise to explain the succession of floors and hearths found beneath the domestic rubbish which filled them. On the other hand the layout of the trenches is obviously defensive. The likeliest answer seems to lie in a change of function from defence to dwelling. This may have happened if the village outgrew its original corner to fill the whole hill-top.

Plate 4 La Starza, Ariano, was like Luni in having natural defences and a long history before Apennine Culture folk built their settlement on it; like Belverde, occasional skeletons have been found among the tumbled rocks round its slopes; like Perto-sa, its material belongs to the Campanian version of the Apennine Culture. Its distinctive importance, apart from the sheer quantity of cultural remains recovered in the course of quarrying and later excavation, lies in its position and its history.

The implication of its site, commanding one of the three lowest passes across the Apennine watershed, has been several times pointed out. Its inhabitants must have had an interest in trade as well as in food production. This is fully borne out by the evidence of the pottery. Though this is Campanian Apennine, a local speciality was the great popularity of excised decoration, in which bands of clay were cut out of the vessel's surface and replaced by an inlay of white paste. This is not surprising since the potters, living on a hill of gypsum, had an unlimited supply of raw material from which to make the paste, plaster of Paris in fact. This ware with cut-out bands is found much more frequently on Apennine sites in northern Campania and northern Apulia than elsewhere in the peninsula, though less commonly than at Ariano itself. It is no doubt due to influence, or indeed import, from Ariano in the pass between the two. In the Late Bronze Age recognisable Apulian traits and objects of bronze from even further afield were brought up the track from the Adriatic coast, some being passed on to Campania.

The site's history was revealed by 16 feet of stratified rubbish deposits on a terrace on its slope. The settlement itself would have been on the summit of the hill, where part of a single hut with a hearth, earthen floor and a post-hole were indeed found. Between the levels with undecorated early Apennine pottery and those with definite Late Bronze Age material were ones with the characteristic band decoration. There was nothing to suggest here, or on any other Italian site, that this was developing locally. It seems clearly adopted from somewhere outside the country.

The important site of Coppa Nevigata, a low hill on the shore of what was then the estuary of the Candelaro River, had lain vacant from the Early Neolithic until the Middle Bronze Age, when it was resettled by people with a culture very similar to that of Ariano. In the Late Bronze Age it came under strong influence from both southern Apulia and the Marche. Details of excavations some years ago should, when published, document the changes. In particular, the unique stone-built defensive wall, 21 feet thick, with its postern opening needs dating.

Sea trade up, down and across the Adriatic from this site is well attested in the Late Bronze Age. If it could be confirmed for this earlier period (and the siting of the settlement on so convenient a harbour would seem to be conclusive) the appearance of dotted band decoration and its variants would be no problem. Seafarers could have brought them across from Yugoslavia, where at Butmir and Vinča closely comparable designs had long been known.

There are some hints that the band decoration reached Italy further north, perhaps instead of, perhaps as well as, at Nevigata. For example, the variety of band filled with laddering or hatching is almost unknown in the south but common on Apennine sites in the Marche and at Belverde, as it is east of the Adriatic. The Early and Middle Bronze Age is yet imperfectly known in Central Italy, being eclipsed by the wealth of Apennine material of the Late Bronze Age. The best documented site is the Grotta a Male, Assergi, already mentioned for its seasonal occupation. As at Nevigata, a Middle Bronze Age level was stratified below others of later date. Its pottery was again decorated and, excepting the absence of the tongue handle, not unlike that of the south. Only later did the elaborate handles of the northern Apennine groups become common. Noteworthy was the discovery here of a mould for casting two flanged axes, proof that the rarity of bronze at this time may be more apparent than real.

The last site for special mention can claim to be the most important of the period in Italy, although only a proportion of its valuable evidence was recovered during its excavation. This is the Scoglio del Tonno (Tunny Reef), a name which is now too widely accepted to be displaced by the more accurate

Plate 51

Fig. 39

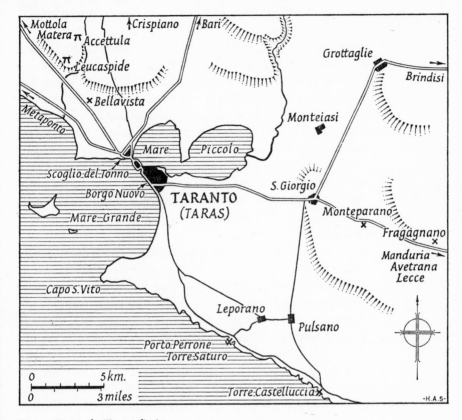

Fig. 39. Sites in the Taranto district

Punta del Tonno. It was a headland which projected into the waters of Taranto harbour, the finest natural harbour on the Italian mainland. The archaeological remains were found and excavated when the modern port was being extended in 1899, the whole headland then being cut away. After a brief occupation in the Late Neolithic, the site had held a fishing and trading settlement from the Middle Bronze Age until the Greek colony of Taras was founded close by, towards the end of the eighth century. Though interesting remains of rectangular huts were found, no satisfactory stratigraphy was recorded, a major tragedy since throughout its life the site had been in constant touch with the Aegean. The well-dated pottery imported from the east could have provided an invaluable time scale for the Italian Bronze and Iron Ages. As it is, no correlation between the local and foreign material can be made. Indeed it is only from the imported sherds that one can tell that the site was in occupation as early as the Middle Bronze Age at all.

It is an important moment in Italian prehistory when Mycenaean ships effected the first direct contact with the civilisations of the east. Traces of influence from Middle Helladic Greece have been recognised on Sicily and the Lipari Islands, but the trading post at Taranto goes back only to the Late Helladic, Mycenaean IIIA. From soon after 1400 BC the Mycenaean merchants were calling regularly, some even settling here, until the Aegean world collapsed during IIIC, in the twelfth century. Thereafter the native element in the site's population was left in control. The trade links with the Aegean continued, weakened but unbroken, and others up the Adriatic

Figs. 40, 41

Fig. 40. *Mycenaean sherds from the Scoglio del Tonno, Myc. III A, B and C*

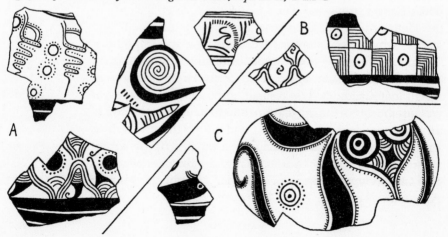

Fig. 41. Mycenaean figurine from the Scoglio del Tonno

were added, a vital factor in the Italian Late Bronze Age.

Local trade through Taranto is shown in several ways. Mycenaean pottery has appeared on two sites in the neighbourhood, Porto Perrone and Torre Castelluccia down the coast to the south-east. It must represent payment for the goods and services which went into the Mycenaean post and shipping at Taranto. Among the pottery types distinctive of this region of the Apennine Culture is one clearly derived from the Aegean, a high loop handle with two small horns added to its apex. It was just the sort of bizarre shape to appeal to the imagination of the Apennine potters, and later spread widely through Italy as a result. A second local handle type, a broad strap drawn up at the upper corners into points, may also have an oriental origin. Otherwise the pottery is a simple variation of southern Apennine Ware.

Fig. 39

Plate 53, *Fig. 38c*

Fig. 38d

125

In the reverse direction, three handle sherds which can only be explained as imports from Apennine Italy were recovered from the corresponding levels at Troy, in the Sixth and Seventh Cities. If not made in Taranto (they are in fact more charac-teristic of the Marche) they were almost certainly shipped through that port.

Mycenaean Taranto could hardly have prospered so greatly on the proceeds of trade with this small corner of Italy alone. Its main function was clearly as a staging point between the Greek homeland, the islands as well as the mainland, and the depots on Sicily, Lipari and beyond. At this point it would be appropriate to examine the whole question of the Mycenaean trade with Italy. Sicily lies rather outside our scope. Geograph-ically Lipari does also, but on settlement sites of the Milazzese Culture there, imported Campanian Apennine and Mycenaean pots were found associated. Rare sherds have come to light also

Fig. 52

on Apennine sites up the west coast, at Castiglione on Ischia, on the islet of Vivara near by and at Luni. What were the Mycenaean traders after?

South-east Sicily was a culturally advanced area in the Cas-telluccio and Thapsos periods and could well attract trade in its own right. There are even hints of it in the Greek legend of the visit of Minos to Sicily and his subsequent death there. The suggestion that Lipari obsidian was the lure would be more convincing if any of it had been found Mycenaean home sites and if the Aegean had not already an excellent and much more convenient source for this material on Melos. The Ischia and Luni sherds imply casual contact, perhaps with other staging points in their neighbourhoods. The destination of this trade route is not difficult to guess.

The Mycenaeans had a voracious appetite for bronze and, despite the wealth of Cyprus, inadequate supplies. Austria probably traded them some, as there is proof of contacts well up the Adriatic: a Mycenaean ingot from the Dalmatian coast, the adoption of the Mycenaean violin-bow fibula in the Po valley, and a Terramara axe mould from Mycenae itself. The 'ox-hide' ingots from Serra Illixi show not only that the Mycenaeans reached Sardinia but that they were probably exploiting its metal ores. And putting the evidence of the Luni sherds alongside that of the Early to Middle Bronze Age hoards to its immediate north, it seems that they were at the very least interested in Tuscan copper sources too. Castiglione and Lipari would now both fall into place, the latter the point where the two routes, from Tuscany and Sardinia, met before continuing together via the Straits of Messina to Taranto and Greece.

The characteristics of the Middle Bronze Age then were vigorous local development contemporary with but, outside the Gulf of Taranto, virtually unaffected by, the contacts with the Aegean world. It was not until the Mycenaeans had ceased to call, when the initiative had passed to the Tarentines, that the widening outlook they had represented began to alter seriously the Apennine Culture and its people.

LATE BRONZE AGE

Two events herald the Late Bronze Age in the peninsula, both occurring within a few years of 1150 BC. In the south, the Mycenaean merchant ships ceased to call at the Scoglio del Tonno. It was a period of upheaval for the Greeks, when all their energies were needed to defend their homes, often without success. The native Tarentines were quick to realise the opportunities thus offered them, of taking over the sea trade in Italian waters as a going concern. The west coast was made difficult for them by the fall of Lipari to a hostile tribe, but there was increasing scope for profitable ventures up the Adriatic coast. This was due to changes in the north. About this time Apennine settlers moving up the corridor between the mountains on the one hand and the Adriatic and Po swamps on the other

Fig. 32

entered Emilia and made peaceful contact with the established culture of the *terremare* in the neighbourhood of Bologna.

A *terramara* is, in the local dialect, a low mound of rich soil. Many were found in the middle Po valley. When they were dug into during the last century for spreading as fertiliser on the fields, it was found that they had been built up by the accumu-lation of domestic refuse on long-lived settlement sites of the Bronze Age. At first their significance was greatly exaggerated, their occupants being regarded as the earliest true Italians. The rest of Italy was dismissed contemptuously as the territory of the *extraterramaricoli,* 'those who dwelt outside *terremare'*. A fairer assessment still allows the Terramara Culture enough impor-tance to the later prehistory of the country to justify some account of it here, although it lay outside the limits of the peninsula.

The Terramara folk entered Italy from the north-east during the Middle Bronze Age, coming from the area of the middle Danube. They brought with them three distinctive cultural features. Their pottery was a dark burnished ware decorated with bosses and grooves and horned handles of a different type, the *ansa lunata,* with flatter pillar and horns. They had learnt before leaving Hungary the skills of bronze-working, which they continued to practise in their new homes. And they in-troduced into Italy the rite of cremation burial, the ashes of the dead being buried in simple jars in urnfield cemeteries close to the settlements. When a deterioration in climate set in, tim-ber-laced earthen ramparts were added to the villages as a pro-tection against floods. The preservation of wood in the damp ground goes some way to explain the original belief that the *terremare* were 'pile-dwellings on dry land'.

The factor which linked these two events in the south and north was the Terramara metal industry. Hitherto the Myce-naeans had been concerned only in carrying metal back to the Aegean, the Tuscan industry was stagnant and the Terramara smiths were relying on metal from the north, the Austrian Alps

Fig. 38b

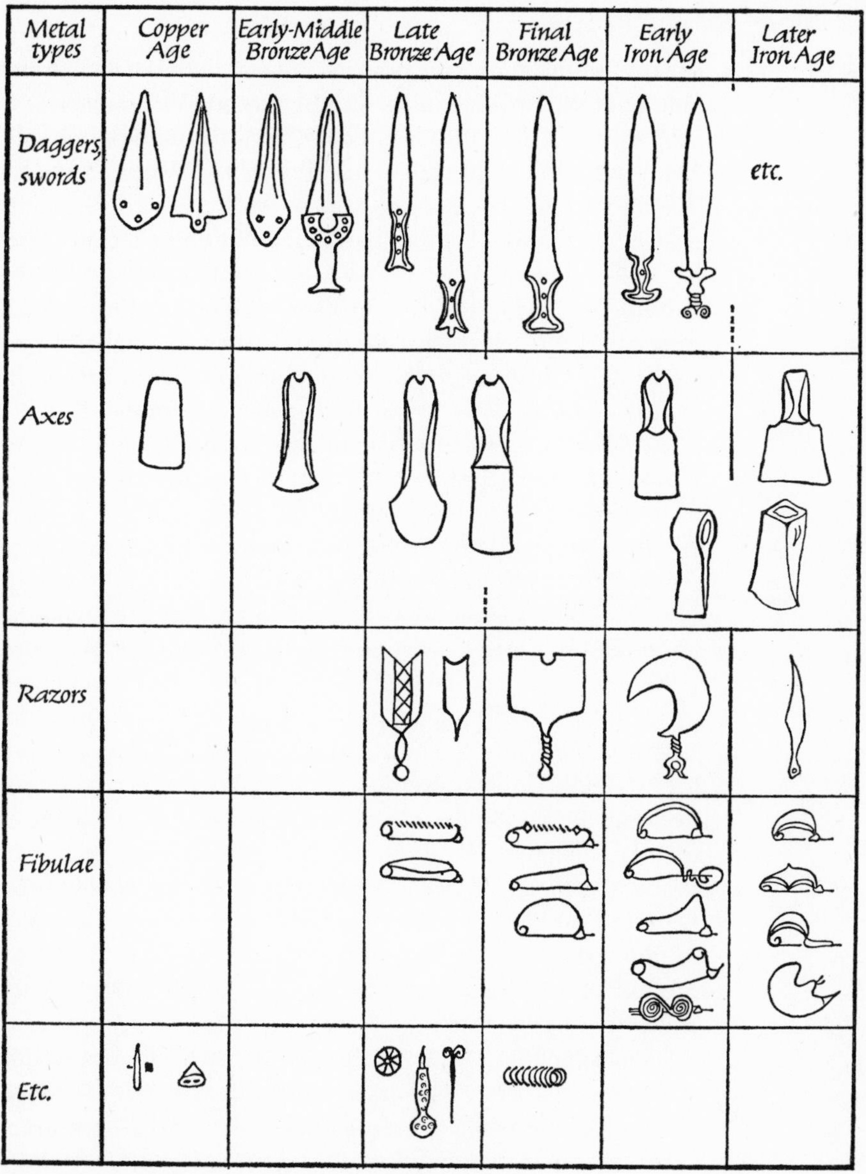

Metal types	Copper Age	Early-Middle Bronze Age	Late Bronze Age	Final Bronze Age	Early Iron Age	Later Iron Age
Daggers, swords						etc.
Axes						
Razors						
Fibulae						
Etc.						

Fig. 42. Development of the metal types in Italy. Not to scale

129

or beyond. Now with the disappearance of the Mycenaeans and the opening of contact between the Terramara and Apennine spheres, the raw bronze of Tuscany became available to the workshops of Emilia. There it was turned into tools, weapons and ornaments, the finished articles being traded by land to Tuscany and perhaps the Marche, and by sea in Tarentine craft to markets down the whole Adriatic coast of Italy. This picture is supported by the date and distribution of metal objects in the south. Those of the Middle Bronze Age are few, concentrated almost entirely in Tuscany and of Tuscan types. Of the Late Bronze Age there are many, particularly in Emilia, Tuscany (Belverde above all), the Marche and east-coast harbour sites like Coppa Nevigata and the Scoglio del Tonno. They are all of recognisable late Terramara forms: winged axes, Peschiera daggers, wheel pendants and violin-bow fibulae with twisted backs, to mention a few examples only.

Fig. 42

Other skills besides metalworking were being adopted by the Apennine folk. From this date their band decoration declined steadily in popularity, to be replaced by the new technique of grooving. At the same time the use of bone increased greatly, a decoration of compass-incised circles being almost a Terramara trademark. The distribution of these was very similar to that of the metal objects. In the reverse direction, many traits in later Terramara pottery were direct borrowings from the Apennine potters after the moment of contact. Particularly noticeable was the high loop handle with small horns springing from it, the type we noted being adopted at Taranto from an Aegean or Trojan form. Emilia in the Late Bronze Age was a region of fruitful cultural fusion.

Plate 61

Fig. 38

The Apennine sites there are mainly open villages in the level plain or overlooking it, like Toscanella Imolese and Monte Castellaccio on either side of Imola. In the rich plains of the Po valley, arable farming must have played a major part in the economy. The frequent discovery of bronze sickles is confirmation of this. The Grotta Farneto, closer to Bologna and in the cf. Plates 59, 60 lower foothills, implies a continuing interest in pastoralism. The *Fig. 59* huts were of the simplest construction, shallow depressions in the ground floored with beaten clay, walled with wattle-and-daub and probably roofed in thatch. At Toscanella a cemetery was found, containing rows of skeletons extended on their backs and unaccompanied by grave goods.

Influence from the *terremare* was most clearly apparent in the metalwork. Not only were all their metal types present, but there was conclusive evidence for the local adoption of the industry in the shape of stone moulds, terracotta crucibles and Plate 60 the like. It is not possible to distinguish the products of these villages from those of the *terremare,* but if the Apennine folk of this region were not making the bronze objects found in the south, they must at least have had a hand in the trade which passed through their territory. At an unlocated port somewhere near Rimini, the precursor of Etruscan Spina, they were traded with the merchants of Taranto, who shipped them south.

Belverde too grew suddenly rich by controlling the supplies of the raw metal from Monte Amiata. In no other way can it have accumulated such wealth of bronzework.

The most important site in the Marche at this time was Santa Paolina near Filottrano, south of Ancona, though the Grotta Frasassi on the Sentino, the Grotta Sant'Angelo inland from *Fig. 45* the Vibrata and the Grotta a Male at Assergi have also produced large quantities of material. Filottrano, unlike these, was an open village of oval huts. An unusual feature on the site was a large rectangular clay-lined pit, apparently a water tank to tide the stock over the period of summer drought when the River Musone below dried up. Antler mattocks attest both Plate 62 agriculture and hunting. As at Toscanella, a flat cemetery was found near by, the skulls showing a mixture of long and round heads similar to that previously noted from the Copper Age tombs.

Plate 61

Bronze and bonework testified to trade with Emilia. The pottery on the other hand was nearly all in the local tradition and marked the peak of flamboyance reached by the Apennine potters. This manifested itself in two ways. The two-dimensional band decoration proliferated but by now there was little scope for further artistic advance in this medium. On some sites, indeed, it began to drop out of favour, probably for that reason. Not so in the three-dimensional field offered by the handles; here the craftsmen, or women, could explore even further the play of curves and solids, achieving results often strange, some-

cf. Plate 63

times unquestionably beautiful. The oddest of these developments occurred not, as one might expect, on the northern class of handle which included the axe, horned, knobbed, crested

Fig. 38
Fig. 37

and other versions of elaborated strap handle, but in a variety of the tongue handle introduced at this time from the south. It consists of two wide-sweeping crescents set back to back on the rim of a bowl, and is the only type of handle which may itself bear the two-dimensional decoration, although elaborate handles are often found on band-decorated vessels. It is also the only type of southern tongue handle to be adopted in the northern half of the peninsula.

The ancestry of the Filottrano handle has become clearer recently with the discovery of intermediate forms on the site of Ariano. A variety of the normal tongue handle was found in the Middle Bronze Age levels, in which the curved sides

Fig. 37

were given a flat bevel confluent with the bowl's rim. On examples from higher deposits, the edges of the bevel converge to a point first at the rim, later slightly above it. The change could be dated to the beginning of the Late Bronze Age by its association with the first evidence for contacts with the north. Notable amongst these was a violin-bow fibula with twisted back which was certainly produced in a workshop in the Po valley. From this type of handle, the progressive exaggeration of the curved bevel and the raising of its lower point into a horn comparable with the upper tip, together with a shortening and broadening of the tongue, led directly to the typical Filottrano handle. Occasional intermediate forms have been found on sites in the Abruzzi, Assergi and Penne for example.

It is dangerously easy in describing this kind of typological development to make it appear as if the handles were themselves responsible for the changes they underwent, or, hardly better, were obeying some impersonal evolutionary instructions. In fact, of course, the motivation could come only from their makers. Since there is no obvious functional advantage in the latest of these handles over the earliest, the changes can be summed up in the one word, fashion. The point is an important one as it throws so interesting a sidelight on the potters, experimenting with curves to produce shapes which came progressively nearer to satisfying their creative urge.

These developments are useful to the archaeologist in another way, by clearly demonstrating cultural relationships. The Filottrano handle is inconceivable without the southern tongue handle and the transitional forms. The 'Ausonian' tongue handle is similarly related. The change of ownership of the Lipari Islands was briefly noticed above. The new occupants were a people whose origins are puzzling. The Middle Bronze Age village on the Citadel of Lipari, like all the others in the islands, was destroyed. It was replaced by another with completely different material, though undoubtedly belonging to a branch of the Apennine Culture.

Professor Brea links it with the legend recorded by Diodorus Siculus of the Ausonian expedition from Campania to occupy Lipari. Its pottery connects it much more closely with regional groups higher in the peninsula and on the Adriatic side. The northern elaborate handles were very popular in both areas, and the only tongue handles of the Late Bronze Age in Lipari are related to those of Ariano and Filottrano, not to the ones current in Campania and elsewhere in the south. They too have the double curve to the sides of the tongue but lack the bevel and the squatness of the peninsular ones. The closest in form are the few examples from the Abruzzi, in which region other parallels to the 'Ausonian' material may one day be found. What remains completely unexplained is the total absence of any sort of decoration on the pottery of Lipari of this phase. The problem of who were Diodorus's Ausonians will become clearer when we come to consider the Final Bronze Age of this area.

The Scoglio del Tonno epitomises the commercial bustle of the Late Bronze Age, a wealthy community with widespread contacts and influence. A continuing trickle of trade with the Aegean is proved by the finding of occasional sherds of Sub-Mycenaean and Proto-Geometric pottery. From Northern Italy came a flood of new ideas to be incorporated in the local pottery, elaborate handles and grooved decoration being the most obvious. More bronzework was found here than on any Apennine site south of Emilia, with the possible exception of Belverde. It included such characteristic Terramara forms as the axe with hafting wings near the centre of the sides, a dagger with flanges to hold the hilt-plates and a fish-tailed end, a curved single-edged knife with its bone handle finely preserved, a sickle, a double-edge razor with openwork centre, a violin-bow fibula with its back flattened into a leaf shape and a variety of pins. A mould for casting a spearhead implies that some metalworking was carried out on the site, probably only for the recasting of scrap metal.

Beside the elaborate handles of the north, the tongue handles and other basic Southern Apennine forms continued to be produced. There was no question of cultural surrender or foreign occupation. Further influence from the east is shown by the fact that, although the painted and wheel-turned wares were no longer being imported in such quantity, they were now being locally imitated. This new ware is particularly associated with

Fig. 43. Decorated bronze pin of Terramara type from the Scoglio del Tonno

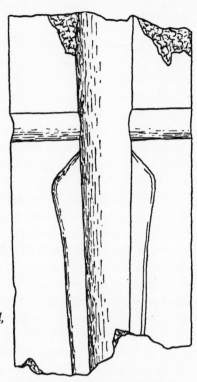

Fig. 44. Mould for casting a spearhead, Scoglio del Tonno

the site of Torre Castelluccia and was to become of greater importance in the Iron Age. In view of the small size and simplicity of the site on the Scoglio del Tonno, one cannot yet talk of civilisation, but its cultural complexity implies that it was nearer that level than any which had preceded it in Italy.

Fig. 39

Coppa Nevigata also flourished exceedingly, though never to rival Taranto. The mound was partly demolished early in this century to build dykes for reclamation work round the Lago Salso, all that remains of the good harbour which had marked the site out for a share in the Adriatic trade. The violin-bow fibula from Ariano must have passed this way. Quantities of pottery and bronze were recovered then, and subsequently even more material reached the museums from proper excavations.

Fig. 38

Plate 14

It showed a similar mixture of local, southern and northern influences. The speciality here was a crested handle with large bosses on either face of the crest, developed from a type imported from the north.

A contrast is provided by the Grotta Manaccora at Peschi⁄ci, 30 miles north⁄east of Nevigata. It is an impressive site, an enormous cave opening on a sandy beach. The headland above it also bore a settlement in which rectangular hut foun⁄dations were recognised. Some cultivable land was to be found near by, there would be unlimited grazing and hunting in the forests of the Gargano inland and fish are plentiful in the sea before it. Though also on the Adriatic coast, this site had as harbour only the open beach and, being cut off by the wild tract of the Gargano, lacked a hinterland. The Adriatic trade therefore passed it by. It showed an impoverished version of the later Apennine Culture of Nevigata with only a few traces of other influences.

The surprising feature was the contents of a cleft or fissure sealed by the earlier levels of the deposit. It had been walled off to serve as a burial place, though none of the actual bones had survived owing to the deleterious effect of the salt from the sea near by. The grave goods, however, included no less than twenty⁄one swords, with other objects of bronze. These too were badly corroded, only four swords being substantially com⁄plete. This wealth of bronze has never been satisfactorily ex⁄plained on a site otherwise so poor.

Italian bronze swords fall into two categories, leaving very few exceptions (a spike⁄tanged example from the Scoglio del Tonno was one). Both have stout blades with long flat tangs flanged along the sides to hold the hilt⁄plates. In one the hilt is forked, sometimes with an additional projection at the cen⁄tre; in the other it expands into an oval or semicircular pommel with the flange continuous round it. The first of these is derived from the fish⁄tailed Peschiera dagger, a product therefore of

Plate 59
Fig. 42

Northern Italy. Three of the Manaccora swords and three from
Belverde were of this type. The fourth Manaccora sword be⁄
longs to the second category, which became the standard form
in the Iron Age. Its origin is a matter of sharp controversy, local,
trans⁄Alpine, trans⁄Adriatic, Aegean and Near Eastern sour⁄
ces all having been suggested. It must for the moment remain
an open question.

FINAL BRONZE AGE

The final stages of the Bronze Age had a completely different
character from anything that had gone before. They formed in
many respects a transition to the Iron Age, when the distinctive
features of the Apennine Culture were fast weakening but the
characteristics of the Iron Age cultural groups which succeeded
it had yet to develop. It is the total absence of iron from the de⁄
posits which makes it a Final Bronze Age rather than a Proto⁄
Iron Age. The name of Proto⁄Villanovans does less than jus⁄
tice to these people, since they played as important a part in the
formation of the other Iron Age peoples, the Latians, Picenes
and the rest, as in that of the Villanovans themselves, as will be
shown in the next chapter. The alternative name for the period,
the Pianello horizon, avoids this difficulty, but horizon in ar⁄
chaeological parlance implies a brief duration, belied by the
number of burials in the Pianello and other urnfields.

The appearance and wide spread of the cremation burial rite
is the most obvious change. Urnfield cremation was introduced
to the Po valley from Hungary by the bearers of the Terramara
Culture around the middle of the second millennium, and soon
became well established. When it was adopted in the peninsula
towards the year 1000 BC, no source further afield need be
sought unless it is demanded by the associated traits.

The ashes of the dead were collected after burning and de⁄
posited in a pottery urn provided with a lid. The jars were

Plate 64

137

variable in form in early and remote cemeteries like Pianello and Timmari but tended to become much more standardised in later ones like Allumiere. There they were nearly all roughly biconical, with everted lips and horizontal handles. Decoration consisted of grooved chevrons and occasional dimples or bosses. The earlier form of lid was a carinated bowl with a high strap handle. Later in the period the use of an open bowl with inturned lip and single horizontal handle became almost universal. All these forms can be paralleled in either the peninsula or the Po valley in the Late Bronze Age. The decoration is more specifically Terramara, the lids and urns Apennine. The Terramara urns were of more globular shapes.

With the ashes were found a few personal possessions of bronze, which tell on the whole a similar story. By far the commonest finds are fibulae and razors. The most popular of the large decorative safety pins now was the arc fibula, with a *Fig. 57* semicircular bow. It was a type new to Italy, obviously imported from outside. At the same time there were three developments of the old violinbow fibula which were certainly local. In one the straight bow was cast with a knob at either end of it. In the second the bow, instead of running parallel to the pin, diverged from it, needing an angle and a longer stalk to the catchplate to hold the latter in the right position to take the tip of the pin, the socalled elbowed form. The third had the *Plates 59, 66* bow flattened into a thin leaf shape, often decorated. An earlier example of this foliate fibula has already been noticed at the Scoglio del Tonno.

Fig. 42 The razors differed from those of the Late Bronze Age but again not so markedly that they could not have been locally developed. They were large and almost square, with a loop handle and a notch in the opposite end. The two sides formed the cutting edges. The Terramara razor had the loop handle and the two edges, but an openwork panel divided the blade into two. The notch may be a relic of this. The main difference is one of technique. The Terramara razor was cast in an open mould, as is shown clearly by the openwork panel, whereas the Pianello one was cut from sheet metal, which does not lend itself to openwork.

A much fuller description of the bronzework of the period is possible from the Coste del Marano hoard, discovered in 1880 at Tolfa in the hills above Civitavecchia, not far from the Allumiere urnfield. It included some 150 pieces, of which the cups and fibulae are the most instructive.

The three cups are of beaten bronze measuring 6 inches in diameter, with designs of repoussé bosses. On the more ela- borate ones the handle is surmounted by a vigorously model- led horned bull's head. These cups are magnificent objects. The eleven fibulae were of three types. Four were of the foliate form, all decorated with bosses, punched dots or engraving on the leaf back and the catchplate. On the two larger exam- ples appeared double sling motifs involving three bosses on one, four on the other. The latter had in addition a variation of these motifs pointing forward to the bird, boat and sun- disc motif, in which a boss rests in a curve having a serifed loop at either end. The second type had two leaf expansions on its back separated from each other, the catchplate, and the spring by figure-of-eight loops. The leaves were again dot-embossed. The third and commonest type was the simple arc fibula. The rest of the hoard was less interesting. Sixteen variously rayed openwork discs had either a loop at one side for suspension or a socket at the centre to be mounted like a wheel. A few other pendants were flat, semicircular or paddle-shaped and usually decorated. Simple armbands, rings and finger spirals were fre- quent. In addition to these decorative objects were a winged axe, a pair of tweezers and various hooks, spikes, needles and pins.

This appears to fall into the category of personal hoards, the possessions of an individual, here a very wealthy one, buried for

Plate 67

Plate 66

safety in a time of troubles or for some other reason. It therefore has more value as a closed group than either a votive hoard or a collection of scrap bronze for melting down. The Pertosa hoard already mentioned contained several pieces of this date, but being votive and deposited over a long period of time it tells us virtually nothing.

The cups of the Coste del Marano hoard provide the strongest evidence for connections with Central Europe, being without any doubt imports from beyond the Alps. They are of the type named after one found at Jenšovice in Bohemia, whence they were distributed within the triangle between Lyons, Denmark and Rumania. However, nothing else in this hoard is of ne-cessity of foreign manufacture. The arc fibulae are a foreign form, as mentioned already, but were certainly being made in Italy. Their origin is in Sub-Mycenaean Greece, where they occur frequently in the Kerameikos cemetery at Athens. They appear in Central Europe only at a later date, as a reflex of the trade which brought the Jenšovice cups south.

The foliate fibulae are Italian works, as are the winged axe and the rayed pendants. All derive from types being turned out by the Terramara craftsmen. Indirectly the double sling motif has come from the same source, the intermediate link being provided by Pianello urns. There a grooved double sling is found over two bosses on the shoulder of an urn. This is only a short step from the concentric grooves over Terramara bosses. The adoption of the sling and its derivative the bird, boat and sun-disc in Central Europe is therefore another borrowing from the Italian Final Bronze Age.

Plate 64

The links to east and north offer the only means of dating this period, not an easy one because it coincides with the Dark Age which preceded the flowering of Classical Greece. For its start it is tempting to use the round figure of 1000 BC, which must, however, be treated as an approximation. The same ap-plies even more strongly to its end at about 850, since it lingered on in many places to a much later date, becoming ever more Final. Only later in the Iron Age does the Italian chronology again become reliable. Radiocarbon dates of 915 and 825, both ± 80, for material of this phase from Luni fall reasonably within this bracket. A secure date for an early urnfield would be very welcome.

The impact of the Final Bronze Age was most apparent across the upper part of the peninsula. The type site of Pianello di Genga, inland from Ancona, lies on the flat valley floor just before the Sentino plunges into a wild gorge. On the Tyrrhenian side the sites cluster more thickly, though Allumiere in the hills above Civitavecchia is the only one of any size. Cremation urns have been reported also from Ortucchio in the Fucino. In the north Bismantova lies well up the Apennine slopes, Fontanella Mantovano in the flattest part of the Po plain, north of the river. In the south the distribution is markedly discontinuous: Albanito in the Sele plain near Paestum, Timmari on a hilltop west of Matera, Torre Castelluccia on the shores of the Ionian, Tropea on the west coast of Calabria and Milazzo facing it in Sicily. The position of four of these on or close to the sea is unlikely to be accidental. Undoubtedly many more sites remain to be found.

Plate 13

Fig. 29

Figs. 9, 39

The picture emerging from this is that Pianello as a cultural group sprang from a fusion of Terramara and Apennine in Emilia, adopting the burial rite and metal industry of one, the pottery forms and in part the food-producing economy of the other. With the decline of vigour of both parent cultures, there was ample scope for the expansion of small groups of people bearing the new ideas. Across the upper peninsula these were readily accepted by the earlier inhabitants in place of their late Apennine traditions. Other groups carried the new ideas to the south by sea but the new fashion in burial rites seems to have been received with much less enthusiasm there. The continuation of the Apennine Culture well into the Iron Age suggests that it was much more firmly entrenched and its people less ready for change. They would be particularly reluctant to give up what is, after all, one of the most conservative of cultural traits, the traditionally approved method of disposal of the dead.

Evidence from Torre Castelluccia is pertinent here. At the gates of a prosperous settlement of Late Bronze to Iron Age date ten cremation urns were discovered. But the fibula and razor found in one of them were both of Late, not Final, Bronze Age type. The two magnificent but unique pins with two spi, rals springing from one side of the head are also much closer to Terramara forms than to any other. This suggests clearly that a small party of people, probably traders, introduced cremation from the Po valley well before its main southward spread. But the local inhabitants held to their ancestral rites (a rock-cut tomb was found near by) and the northerners were either ab, sorbed or returned home, apart from the few buried here. The introduction of cremation elsewhere was probably by similar means.

At Timmari cremation was adopted and remained in use for a very long period. The large number of burials, in marked contrast to Torre Castelluccia, indicates this, and it is con, firmed by the occurrence of a few vessels of a painted ware from Sicily of Iron Age date. The practice of setting stones on the surface to mark the individual graves is also not otherwise known until that later date, becoming quite frequent with the Etruscans.

The material from the cemetery at Milazzo is so indistinguish, able from that at sites like Allumiere or Pianello, that it must be regarded as the burial place of another and rather larger band of expatriate northerners. The rite was translated into local terms in the Piazza Monfalcone cemetery on Lipari. There, inhuma, tion in large jars, an oriental rite introduced through Sicily, gradually gave way to cremation burial in bucket-shaped urns of purely local form. These were buried on their sides (like the large jars), and closed with slabs of stone. There are several departures from the standard rite, but it is difficult to dissociate the appearance of cremation here from the arrival of the urn-fielders at Milazzo.

Lipari gives us a chance to examine the domestic material corresponding to the urnfields. At Torre Castelluccia the burials were probably of an alien minority, to which the material from the settlement was not necessarily relevant. At Timmari the cemetery and its village continued down to so late a date that their evidence for the Final Bronze Age is suspect. On Lipari the Piazza Monfalcone cemetery and the Ausonian II levels on the Citadel overlooking it unquestionably correspond in time. And the Ausonian II domestic material shows a combination of Apennine and Terramara elements very similar to that in the urnfields themselves. The carinated bowls, the horn-ed animal-headed handles, the Trojan type high looped handles and the horizontal handled bowl point to the former, the plentiful use of grooving to the latter.

The closest parallels to this material are in the Early Iron Age cemeteries of Campania (p. 154 below). Final Bronze Age sites have yet to be identified in that region; the corresponding levels further north at Luni certainly have a similar content. The Ausonian II Culture represents another immigration to the Lipari Islands from the peninsula, and one which squares much better with Diodorus's record of the Ausonians. Here we have the first people in Italy to whom we can ascribe a name other than a conventional archaeological fiction.

In the upper peninsula are three sites worth a closer look. At Ponte San Pietro on the Fiora a small urnfield was found at the foot of a hill yielding settlement material. The latter was scanty and impoverished Apennine, but included a fine bronze winged axe of Final Bronze Age form. At Casa Carletti, hut foundations were found on the slope of Monte Cetona a short distance from Belverde but here the burial place was not located.

Plate 5

Plate 68

Plate 11

Plate 65

The hybrid nature of the Pianello material was well summed up in a single vessel, a fine carinated bowl having an Apennine shape and stag's-head handle, and good Terramara grooving on handle and lip.

The most interesting group of sites is that in the thorough-

ly explored Gola del Sentino and neighbourhood. At its head was the type site, the urnfield cemetery of Pianello di Genga, with some hundreds of burials. If Spineto falls into the Middle, and Frasassi and the open site below it, on the evidence of Filottrano, into the Late Bronze Age, one can hardly escape the conclusion that the Final Bronze Age is represented by the deposits in the Grotta del Mezzogiorno (Cave of Noon, or the South) and the Grotta Baffoni. They are within 2 miles of the cemetery, have not produced burials of their own, and show the same mixture and fusion of pottery traits as occur in the urnfield and characterise this period else-where. Here the continuity of settlement, and presumably the economy that that implies, emphasises the Apennine side of the cultural fusion, but the cremation rite and complete replace-ment of band decoration on the pottery by grooves serve as re-minders that the Terramara element played an equal part in its formation.

The use of the sea-ways in the spread of the urnfielders to the south has been mentioned, though the activity on the Adriatic seems to have slackened since the preceding period. Sea trade there certainly was, including lively contact with the Dalmatian

Plate 14

coast opposite. Coppa Nevigata and the Grotta Manaccora were the sites most affected. Many traits at Final Bronze and Iron Age sites in Bosnia, Donja Dolina and Debelo Brdo for example, are derived from antecedents in Southern Italy, often specifically at Nevigata. That site actually yielded little that must be foreign; the Grotta Manaccora on the other hand has a great deal which is unrelated to anything happening in Italy at this time. Its later levels produced a large number of cups

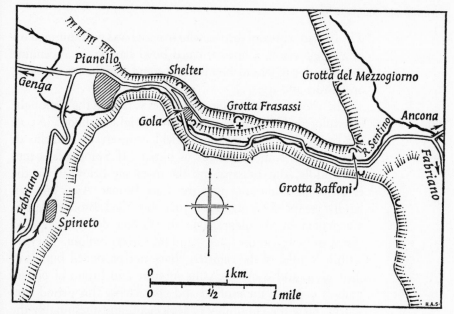

Fig. 45. Sites in the Gola del Sentino, Ancona

and small jars with diagonally facetted shoulders. The similarity to pottery from Dalmatia, particularly from the urnfield at Zaton near Zara, is very striking. Only the quantity of
Apennine traits also present prevents one from regarding it as a
trans-Adriatic colony.

A small group of sites further south introduces another foreign element, the so-called Bisceglie or Bari dolmens. They are
more accurately megalithic Gallery Graves. Five of them are
recorded from the province of Bari, that standing 3 miles inland
from Bisceglie being the best known. There are in addition
four outliers, two near Taranto (Leucaspide and Ricettula)
one in the province of Brindisi and a possible one on the tip
of the Gargano.

Typologically they form a homogeneous group, all consisting of a gallery with parallel sides built of slabs raised on edge

Plate 7
Fig. 9

145

Fig. 46

to support others forming the roof. Sill-stones across the passage are usual and there is no separate chamber. Traces of a mound or cairn are present on several, so damaged or added to in the course of clearing the fields around for cultivation that their original form cannot be guaranteed. The best preserved, Albarosa and San Silvestro, now appear rectangular or oval but both of these are confused by having corbelled field huts,

Plate 8

the Apulian *trulli*, built into them. Where preserved sufficiently to show their size, the chambers are about 35 feet long and 5 to 6 feet wide internally, aligned east-west. San Silvestro, discovered near Giovinazzo in 1961, is exceptional in several respects. It is only $2\frac{1}{2}$ to 3 feet wide but 53 feet long; the end sections of its passage are built in dry stone rubble rather than orthostats; the sill stones rise nearly 2 feet above the floor level; and six capstones of an original nine survive in position, where no other has more than one remaining. Its axis runs north-south, the northern and probable entrance end being flag paved.

Three tombs, Bisceglie, Albarosa and Leucaspide, yielded material, all of late Apennine forms, which is published or accessible in museums. No details of the excavation of San Silvestro are yet available. At Albarosa the finds included one or two sherds of Torre Castelluccia Painted Ware. Amber beads and a small bronze disc from Bisceglie can be paralleled from the rock-cut tombs on Murgia Timone, as can the pottery. Burial was again by inhumation. Of eleven skeletons recovered from Bisceglie, one, presumably the latest, was found articulated in a crouched position. This and the grave goods – other than the amber, of course, – point to local tradition but the tomb type cannot be of local derivation.

Apart from the use of megalithic blocks for tomb-building, these Gallery Graves are quite unlike the Otranto dolmens (see p. 87) in form, distribution or date, and there can hardly be any connection between them. The 'dolmens' of Pian Sultano, on the coast above Rome, are unconvincing in the same three re-

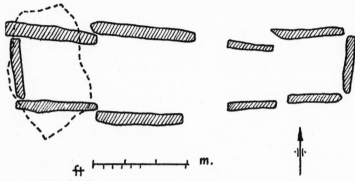

Fig. 46. Plan of Gallery Grave, Bisceglie. Cf. Fig. 27

spects. Apulia being the eastern limit of megalithic tombs in
Europe, one must assume that their builders brought the idea
by sea from the west. Sardinia has Gallery Graves at about this
period, the 'Giants' tombs'. Most have elaborate semicircular
forecourts but simpler, and so more similar, forms do occur.
There are others in Provence and the Pyrenees, of much earlier
date. If there is any connection here, its origin, course, date and
implications remain at present equally baffling. And local derivation from Otranto would leave almost as many problems.

In the south in particular there is no reason to doubt that the
Apennine burial rite of inhumation in trenches or rock crevices
continued. An inurned cremation can easily be attributed to
its period but an unaccompanied skeleton is undatable. At
two sites, burials certainly of this period and in the native tradition have been found, confirming a measure of continuity
through the sweeping cultural changes of the Final Bronze Age.
They are rock-cut chamber tombs, one rather earlier at Torre
Castelluccia and three on the Murgia Timone near Matera, *Figs. 9, 39*
the site which had held the Middle Neolithic ditched village.
Earlier ones to bridge the gap from the Copper Age have yet
to be discovered, though rifled tomb chambers at Altamura
and Gravina a short distance to the north may belong in that

Fig. 47. Spout-handled vase, Murgia Timone

period. The Bronze Age tombs are unlikely to be the result of reimport from some unidentified foreign source in Sicily or elsewhere in view of the local grave furniture.

These tombs contained pure Late Apennine pottery, including carinated tongue-handled bowls, a small jar with a *becco-ansa,* a handle perforated through its length to act as a spout at the same time, and two charcoal hearth fragments. A serpentine fibula belongs early in the Iron Age and implies repeated use down to that late date. Other bronzes, a few glass beads and pieces of amber were less explicit.

So passed the Apennine Culture, lingering in some parts of the country but in most steadily fading away. The cultural poverty of this phase is imparted by the term Sub-Apennine which has come into use recently. It must be used with great caution, however, because of its wide variation in space and time. The more general term of Final Bronze Age has been preferred here. The period is one of decline, but is vitally important as it contained the main seeds of all later developments in the prehistory of the peninsula.

Plate 52
Fig. 47

CHAPTER VI

The Early Iron Age

IRON AS A RAW MATERIAL has many advantages over bronze: its ores are far more common, it can be forged at lower temperatures than are necessary for casting bronze, and the resulting metal is much more durable and will take a keener edge. The reason for its later appearance lies in the complica￾tions of working it. Smelting produces only a spongy and useless mass, the iron bloom. The metal is extracted from this by re￾peated hammering in association with red hot charcoal, which removes impurities and adds the carbon necessary to turn soft iron into a useful steel. This technique was a jealously guarded discovery of the Hittite Empire in the fifteenth century BC, knowledge of it spreading only after the overthrow of the Hit￾tites some two centuries later.

With the introduction of an iron-using economy early in the first millennium, Italy entered upon a period of great prosperity and population increase. The richness of its cemeteries attracted far more attention from the early archaeologists than did the poorer earlier periods, which were also more remote from the main object of their interest, the beginnings of the Greek, Etrus￾can and Roman civilisations. As a result, Italian museums contain more material of this period than of all the rest of pre￾history combined. The wealth of funerary evidence is, however, balanced by a marked shortage of information on the settlement sites, few of which have been investigated.

Discussion must be limited strictly to the Early Iron Age. With the rise of the Etruscans in the centre and the Greek col￾onies in the south, the story soon becomes impossible to follow without constant reference directly or indirectly to the Greek homeland or to the written sources of Greece and Rome. This applies even to the native peoples not immediately subjugated by their more advanced neighbours. The Etruscans and Greeks themselves, and the Romans, soon to become the most important of the Italic peoples, have already been studied in this series. For an account of the preceding period, the primary evidence has to be derived from archaeology rather than by study of the Latin writers' information. Accordingly, any term of nonarchaeological origin like 'Picenes' or 'Daunians' must be accepted with only an archaeological connotation. 'Ausonians' in this sense has already been met with.

The population growth is probably to be explained by an increasing emphasis on agriculture, a more productive economy than the stockbreeding of the Bronze Age. The appearance of the cheaper and more efficient iron tools would assist the process by giving man a greater control over his environment. Coupled with rising population came cultural diversification, regional variants of the Apennine Culture reappearing and becoming rapidly more marked until they have to be regarded as separate cultures.

Fig. 48

INHUMING CULTURES

APULIA

Paradoxically the heel of Italy, which one would expect to be the first to receive new influences coming from the east, remains the most backward region. Dark burnished Apennine Ware, with typical bowl shapes and elaborate handles, survived unaltered at Coppa Nevigata until the site was abandoned. The iron foundry discovered here proves that this was not until well into the Iron Age, when the siltingup of its harbour killed its flourishing sea trade. Similarly the native settlement on the Scoglio del Tonno continued to make its traditional wares until it was replaced by the city of Taras in about 706 BC. Here it was the Greek colonists rather than natural agencies which barred the natives from their port and their livelihood. At Torre Castelluccia a few miles to the southeast, according

Fig. 39

Fig. 48. Iron Age sites and regions

1. Statue menhirs of the Magra valley
2. Bologna (Villanova, S. Vitale, Benacci, etc.). See Fig. 59.
3. Populonia
4. Vetulonia
5. Tarquinia
6. Luni, Monte Romano
7. Veii
8. Rome (Palatine, Forum, etc.)
9. Alban Mountains, (Grottaferrata, etc.)
10. Sermoneta
11. Piediluco (hoard)
12. Le Accieraie, Terni
13. Verucchio, Rimini
14. Novilara
15. Fermo
16. Cupramarittima
17. Alfedena
18. Alife
19. Cumae. See Fig. 52
20. Ischia (Castiglione, Monte Vico). See Fig. 52
21. Val di Sarno
22. Pontecagnano, Salerno
23. Grotta Manaccora, Peschici
24. Coppa Nevigata
25. Timmari. See Fig. 9
26. Taranto (Scoglio del Tonno, Borgo Nuovo, Torre Castelluccia, etc.). See Fig. 39
27. Vanze, Lecce
28. Torre Mordillo
29. Torre Galli, Tropea
30. Locri (Canale, Janchina, Scorciabove)
31. Citadel, Lipari

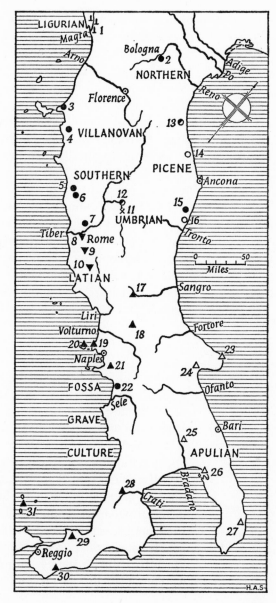

to the preliminary report of the excavation, the local ware continued in use alongside black-slipped Egnatian Ware of the
third century.

Although pottery of pure Apennine type or obvious Apennine derivation certainly persisted throughout the Early Iron
Age, it was gradually replaced by the buff wheel-turned ware
painted in purple-brown and red, known as Apulian Geometric. The origins of this lie in the Torre Castelluccia Ware,
itself copied locally from imported Mycenaean wares. Renewed
influence from Greek Geometric is evident, but the name must
not be taken to imply merely an Italian version of the latter.
At a date beyond the limits of our period the generalised Apulian Geometric Ware split into three separate kinds.

A very useful group of pottery, probably a votive deposit of
the eighth century, is the Pozzo d'Eredità or Borgo Nuovo
hoard, found in a well under the new city of Taranto. It
consists mainly of a wide range of small painted jars which
look back to the Torre Castelluccia Ware and forward to
the much more elaborate Messapian style of the seventh century and later. There are also hints of Greek Geometric. Together with these, however, are a few obvious Apennine vessels,
hand-made, dark burnished, carinated and with axe handles.

The cemeteries of this region are extraordinarily poorly known
considering the wealth of evidence throughout the rest of the
peninsula. There is nothing here to compare with the great
cemeteries of Bologna, Etruria, the Alban Mountains, Novilara,
or even Calabria. A few collective tombs like the Bisceglie
Gallery Graves and the rock-cut chambers of Matera may have
continued in use from the preceding period. The only addition
appears to have been the *specchie,* curious cairns up to 30 feet
across and 6 feet high found over most of Apulia. The best
studied group is between Vanze and Acquarica, 8 miles south-
east of Lecce. Within each cairn was a slab-built dolmenic cist
holding a single crouched skeleton. Traces of an entrance pas-

Plate 71

sage in some of them imply a derivation from the megalithic Gallery Graves, but the rite of collective burial had been completely abandoned. With the skeletons had been placed vessels of an undistinguished degenerate Apennine Ware, and a few fibulae of arc and *serpeggiante* forms place these monuments firmly in the Iron Age.

Fig. 57

Also referred to as *specchie* are much larger loose rubble cairns up to 50 feet high forming prominent landmarks throughout the Salento. They are not yet clearly understood. A circular dry stone wall, either inward- or outward-facing, is usually built into the cairn and buried under further rubble. One at least had an external staircase, suggesting perhaps a watch- tower. No associated pottery or other finds have ever been found in them and occasional sporadic sherds on the buried surface beneath them say only that they cannot be earlier than Iron Age.

Plate 8

Four hoards found in Apulia, together with two from Cala- bria and one near Campobasso, form a group quite distinct from anything higher up the peninsula. The axes, spears, chisels and sickles of which they are composed not only show few signs of use but many had not even been properly finished off. They are therefore merchants' hoards, stocks of new tools being traded by someone part itinerant tinker, part door-to-door salesman. It is significant that the standard Italian winged axe, in which the wings are now attached to the end furthest from the cutting edge, is here almost unknown, however com- mon in the north. A single example came from Manduria, 20 miles east of Taranto. Its successor in the north, the spade- shaped axe, does not occur at all. In their place appears the shaft-hole axe, present in every one of these hoards and in three of them the only tool, yet occurring in only three northern hoards. Beside its one winged and four shaft-hole axes, the Manduria hoard had 103 socketed ones, a form never common in Italy.

Plate 69

Fig. 42

These tools must come from a quite different centre of production and their distribution round the Gulf of Taranto suggests that this lay outside the peninsula. Sicily, which also employed shaft-hole and socketed axes in preference to winged ones, offers the likeliest source.

The impression given by Apulia at this period is one of slow change affecting the way of life of the people only slightly. The archaeological evidence throws little light on the arrival of the Messapian language, thought by philologists to be the latest to reach Italy from the east at about this time. There is equally little presage of the burst of often fantastic development to follow in the Second Iron Age, when the Apulian Geometric Painted Ware sprouted into the Daunian, Peucetian and Messapian varieties in the north, centre and south of Apulia respectively. Though these are definitely local, the Greek colony of Taras must have played its part, by increasing prosperity and introducing new ideas to the local potters. Apulia remains the least studied of all the Iron Age regions of Italy.

FOSSA GRAVE
CULTURE
For the rest of the south the most convenient starting point is Lipari, since no corresponding settlement sites have yet been found on the mainland. Even less change is visible there than in Apulia, the Ausonian II material continuing at least as late as the ninth century, as is shown by a stilted fibula of that date imported from Sicily. Diodorus records a population of five hundred when the Greeks arrived to found their colony in 580 BC, and no prehistoric material later than Ausonian II has been found. It looks therefore as if the destruction of the latest Ausonian buildings should be attributed to the Greeks rather than to unknown raiders who did not stay.

Since the Ausonians came to Lipari from the mainland in the Final Bronze Age, the corresponding Fossa Grave Culture there must have started in that period. By the Iron Age there are many sites in Campania and Calabria. In the south a number of large cemeteries are known, some of trench graves (which

Fig. 49. Fossa Grave pottery from tombs in the Scorciabove cemetry, Locri

give the culture its name) like Torre Mordillo north of Cosenza and Torre Galli near Tropea, some of rock-cut tombs like Canale and Janchina at Locri east of Reggio. The latter are more closely related to the large Sicilian cemeteries, Pantalica for example, than to the Italian ones of Gaudo or Torre Castelluccia. This connection tallies with the evidence of the shaft-hole axes and of the classical traditions of Siculi in the toe of Italy.

The material is plentiful but on the whole not very distinguished. The bronzes include all the main types of fibula to be discussed more fully below, such as the simple arc, the arc with disc catchplate and the *serpeggiante,* as well as spear-heads, knives, arm-bands and other personal possessions. The pottery is mostly plain, still hand-made, dark and burnished. Jars, and curved and carinated bowls, look back to Pianello and Apennine forms; the *askos,* a jar with its neck off-centre, figuring quite largely, must be an introduction from the Ae-

Fig. 57

Fig. 49

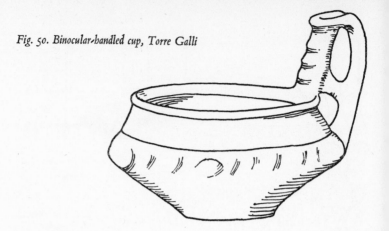

Fig. 50. Binocular-handled cup, Torre Galli

Fig. 50

gean either directly or by way of Sicily. More characteristic of this period are bowls in which a short shoulder above the carination is grooved diagonally or in semicircles over low bosses. The high handle is divided into two openings by a cross-piece, the binocular handle, and its inner bar is often a grooved pillar rather than a strap. It is this form in particular which links Ausonian II Lipari, Calabria and Campania so closely.

Fig. 51

One other distinctive object (it cannot be described as a vessel) needs mention here, a truncated terracotta pyramid with a horizontal perforation through the top. It is widely common and usually considered to be a loom weight. Calabrian examples, especially from the Locri cemeteries, are elaborately decorated with deeply incised or cut-out designs employing meanders and swastikas.

Fig. 51. Decorated loom weights from tombs in the Canale and Janchina cemeteries, Locri

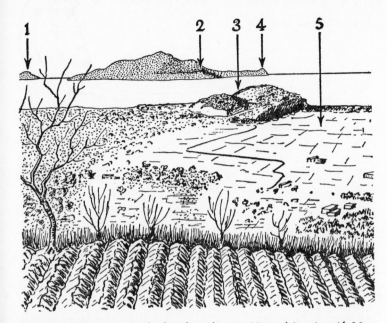

Fig. 52. View of Cumae and Ischia from the north-east 1. Vivara (Apennine with Myce-naean) 2. Castiglione d'Ischia (Apennine and Mycenaean, then Iron Age) 3. The Acropolis of Cumae, Greek Kyme 4. Monte Vico (Iron Age and Greek settlement of Pythecusae) 5. The Cumae cemeteries

The development in the south was cut short by the founda-tion of the Greek colonies all round its coasts, often taking over the native site, as at Locri. Further north, Campania was much less affected. True, the most important site, Cumae, was replaced by a Greek settlement at a comparatively early date but that was the only one on the mainland here. In the Val di Sarno at the foot of Vesuvius the cemeteries only began in the eighth century and continued to a much later date, certainly well be-yond our limits. The great inland cemeteries at Alife and Al-fedena began even later, so they need not concern us. In Roman times a number of tribes were recorded from this area, shar-ing dialects of the Oscan language, a close relative of Latin.

157

Fig. 52

At Cumae the first settlement was founded in the tenth or ninth century on a small isolated hill beside the sea. All traces of it were swept away by later Greek and Roman occupation but, below it to the north, its trench grave inhumation cemetery came to light. The material was basically similar to that of Calabria with some minor differences. The binocular-handled cup, sometimes with a pair of very Apennine or even Trojan horns springing from its top, was particularly common. Arc *Fig. 57* and *serpeggiante* fibulae were both present. The short Iron Age sword with T-pommel occurred in bronze and more rarely in *Fig. 42* iron. An unusual specimen with a single edge and asymmetric handle resembling a cavalry sabre looks more oriental than Italian, but two other examples are known from a Latian cemetery at Sermoneta.

The great importance of the site lies in the significance of its external connections. Long before the Greek colony of Kyme was founded in 750, traders were using the sandy beach and defensible hill overlooking it as a station between the metal-producing regions of Tuscany and Calabria, Sicily and beyond. Plate 70 The Osta 3 tomb at Cumae included a vessel of Greek Geometric manufacture. It is one of the earliest to appear in an Italian context, probably going back to the ninth century BC. The evidence for trade with the Greeks at this early date is vitally important, since they were certainly responsible for the introduction of the knowledge of iron into Italy.

Conversely, the designs of some vessels from this cemetery, particularly square meanders and stylised human figures, have *Fig. 53* clearly been influenced by the Villanovan Culture. The technique used, bands of closely spaced parallel lines, is typical. Other Campanian cemeteries, notably Pontecagnano east of Salerno, show Villanovan influence also. The presence of an occasional cremation burial is less conclusive in itself; but when present in numbers, they look more like a reintroduction than a survival from Pianello times.

Fig. 53. Jar with Villanovan type of decoration, Cumae. (After Gabrici)

For a settlement of this period and region one has to cross to Ischia, facing Cumae and only 8 miles away. The Greek trading post of Pythecusae, now Monte Vico above Lacco Ameno, was the first one in the west since Mycenaean times. It was preceded by a short-lived native village at Castiglione, the rocky hill which had long before supported the Apennine site. Since this immediately antedates the Greek settlement, it must be at least approximately contemporary with the Cumae cemetery. The differences between their material are such as one would expect when comparing domestic and funerary remains. Some sherds again show Villanovan influence in their decoration but most are much coarser wares, very large lugged jars and the like. The site produced the best restorable example of the charcoal brazier common in various forms at this time. It took the form of a large *situla* or bucket with four holes in its base, raised on a high pedestal cut away at the front. Loom weights are common and curious objects with disc-projections have been interpreted as idols.

Fig. 52

Fig. 54

159

Until recently the important Iron Age culture on the east coast, that of the Picenes, was known only from tombs. Excavations within the city of Ancona have now given, if not actual huts, at least stratified deposits of domestic refuse to fill out the picture. These have yielded the coarser kitchen wares, minor tools and domestic animal bones which naturally one cannot expect in the tombs, any more than one can large numbers of fibulae, pendants, spears and swords on a village rubbish tip. The value of domestic deposits is that they give a truer picture of the way of life of a people and in addition allow the development over the period of a site's occupation to be studied in much more detail than is possible in cemeteries. Though each grave illustrates one moment in time, it is rarely easy to sort all the graves present into chronological order.

The earliest levels here have revealed several important links between Picene and the preceding Bronze Age material. Two examples will suffice to demonstrate this. A very common

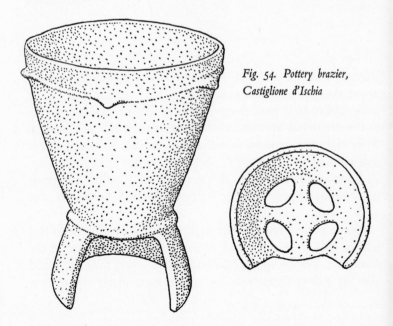

Fig. 54. Pottery brazier, Castiglione d'Ischia

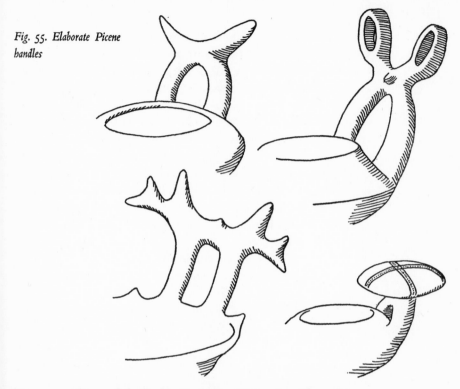

Fig. 55. Elaborate Picene handles

Picene vessel is a globular bowl with a bridge handle arching above the rim and having a wide splayed semicircular flange at its apex. It is now securely linked by intermediate forms to the in-curved lip bowl with horizontal handle of Pianello. More elaborate versions in which the handles become pairs of stylised deer obviously owe much to Apennine traditions also. A bone awl handle from the Ancona site would have given no cause for surprise on a late Apennine or even Terramara one, its decoration of compass-incised circles being of identical type.

Picene pottery remains the dark *impasto* ware current in this part of Italy since the Ripoli *figulina* went out of fashion in the Neolithic. The liking for curious handles is very noticeable and also has a long ancestry in the region. Particularly common is

Fig. 55

Central and Southern Italy

Plate 75

Fig. 57

Fig. 57

one in which a large decorated disc is set on the top of a small bridge handle, the whole standing on the shoulder of a broad vase. Another looks extraordinarily like a half-opened pair of scissors attached to the vessel by the blade tips. A simple geo-metric decoration is often worked in grooving or by pressing a cord into the soft pot surface before the firing, a technique wide-spread also in the Villanovan Culture and in Italy confined to this period.

The locally derived pottery is balanced by other traits which suggest close links with the opposite coast of the Adriatic. These could imply more than mere trade relationships. For example, the spectacle fibula, in which the bow comprises two large flat spirals, has its origin in what is now Yugoslavia. It was very popular with the Picenes but hardly occurs elsewhere in Italy. Also the Picene language, as recorded in later inscriptions, is related to Illyrian, the Indo-European language of Dalma-tia. Some elements of Picene culture are foreign, many are local, and the proportion of the two in its make-up will only become apparent after much more careful research. The prob-lem is very similar to that of the Etruscans, at which we must glance shortly.

The most famous of the many cemeteries are those of Novi-lara, in the hills 4 miles south of Pesaro. The earlier or Molaroni cemetery, called after the owner of the property on which it was found, at first gave some difficulty in dating since the simple arc fibula elsewhere characteristic of the Final Bronze and opening stages of the Iron Ages never became popular among the Pi-cenes. Instead was found a confusing mixture of fibulae: exam-ples of violin-bow type which one would expect to be early, boat-shaped ones of a much later type and spectacle fibulae rare outside the Marche at any period. Molaroni probably runs parallel to the earlier Villanovan cemeteries at Bologna in the eighth century. The Servici cemetery near by began in the following century and both continued in use until very much

162

later, characterised by the fibulae with lengthened catchplates.

A distinctive feature of Picene cemeteries of all dates was the prevalence of amber. It was popular for beads, spindle whorls, pendants, great disc-shaped ear-rings, or threaded onto arc fibulae to produce the boat outline in either a single lump or a graduated series of rings. Ivory was exceptionally, bone more often, used in the same ways. Bronze was common throughout, much of it of Villanovan manufacture. More characteristic are long pendants consisting of engraved trapezoidal plates with ducks' heads at the upper corners supporting bronze chains. They were worn hanging from the waist. For weapons, however, bronze was soon replaced by iron. Slashing swords and spearheads were very common.

Plate 75

Plates 75, 77

These wide-ranging contacts, bronze from Tuscany, amber from the Baltic, ivory from Africa, the spectacle fibulae from the Balkans, prove that the Picenes were traders as well as farmers. We are fortunate in having a picture of their ships engraved on a stele from the Novilara cemetery of about the sixth century, later but still relevant. It is a long, low craft with a single mast and square sail. A vividly portrayed crew bends to its oars (though only four of these are shown), urged on by

Fig. 56

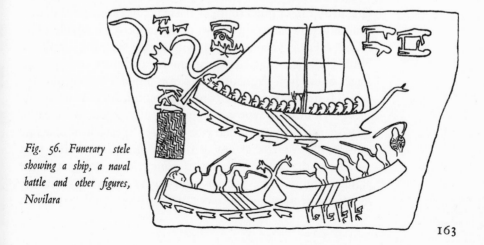

Fig. 56. Funerary stele showing a ship, a naval battle and other figures, Novilara

163

a standing figure at the foot of the mast. At the stern sits the steersman with his oar. The bows project into a ram below the water line and a high figurehead above. Beneath it are shown two more ships in fierce conflict. The line between trade and piracy was in those days a fine one. War was not the only danger to be feared. Even earlier (eighth century) is a Late Geometric Greek vase from Ischia showing a shipwreck, the vessel upside down in the waves and its crew swimming for their lives.

A rich woman's grave of the seventh century was transferred bodily from Novilara to the Pigorini Museum in Rome and only recently properly re-excavated. It well illustrates not only the wealth of the Picenes but also the manner in which they wore it. On the woman's head were traces of a thin bronze diadem probably holding a head-cloth, though the fabric had of course disappeared. To this, it seemed, a veil had been attached by means of two small fibulae, found on either temple. Suspended from either ear were three large amber discs, each measuring 2 inches across. A scatter of small glass and bone beads in great numbers spoke of an elaborate necklace kept extended on her breast by two circle-decorated bone spacer plates. Her right sleeve was trimmed with a row of diamond-shaped bone pendants hanging from bronze rings; her left sleeve had trapezoidal ones of amber and two sea-shells. She wore a bronze bracelet and a ring on the middle finger of her left hand. There were two bronze chain pendants. The smaller looked as if it had been attached to the left elbow by a large fibula, but it may have been placed on the body afterwards rather than worn in this position. The larger was attached to a belt, the bronze fastening of which lay near it. It hung over the left hip, its pendant chains reaching a little below the level of the knee. Three large iron rings and several small bronze ones by the left foot may have been worn as anklets and toe rings but were no longer round the bones.

Plate 75

We would give a great deal to know the appearance of the rest of her attire, the parts like her head-cloth and dress which have not survived the centuries. With her lay others of her possessions, which add to our picture of her in life – ten pottery vessels of various forms, a decorated spindle whorl and three bobbins for thread, all in terracotta, a nest of six large iron rings and a curious bronze and bone pendant, two small ornaments in the shape of horses and a great variety of fibulae, from 2 to 8 inches long, with bronze, amber or ivory bows.

The distribution of this culture covers almost exactly the present-day region of the Marche. There was some intermingling with the Villanovans on all sides. To the north-west there was a mixed cemetery at Verucchio, inland from Rimini; to the south-west southern Umbria seems to have been occupied by a genuine hybrid group. In the reverse direction a group of Villanovans penetrated to the heart of Picene territory, to leave a typical urnfield at Fermo within sight of the Adriatic and the Picene cemetery of Cupramarittima. Southwards there was a little overflow into the Abruzzi but the Iron Age of that region is very inadequately known.

Plates 78, 79

The best known Iron Age cemetery in Umbria was discovered when the steelworks, Le Accieraie, were erected at Terni in the 1880's. Traces of huts were found also but received little study. The material shows influence from the Picenes to the east and the Villanovans to the west. Both forms of burial were present but it is an over-simplification to suppose that an inhumation grave must be the resting place of a Picene and a cremation grave that of a Villanovan since the associated finds did not always tally, and were indeed often unlike those of either. For example, the presence of circular settings of stones round the graves is peculiar to this group. Simple mixture is not the only answer; we have here a genuine cultural group, albeit hybrid in origin and of comparatively minor importance to the prehistory of the country.

UMBRIANS

The pottery adds to this picture. It is rather generalised and helps to emphasise the fact that behind the specialised types in each region, the Campanian binocular handled cup, the Picene elaborated bridge handle, the Villanovan storeyed urn, the Latian reticulatecordoned jar, there is a common background of material which can be classed only as Italian Iron Age. The same applies to much of the metalwork: the razors, both the earlier rectangular and the later lunate forms, the short Iron Age sword and the socketed spearhead are common to all areas. Fibulae are more distinctive, since nowhere else in Italy did the disc fibula achieve such popularity. In it the catchplate is expanded into a disc of spiral form sometimes preceded by a transverse bar. These lay at right angles to the plane of the fibula and were often given a delicate engraved decoration by the craftsmen who made them. The bow of the fibula could assume as wide a variety of forms as in those with the standard catchplate (see p. 175)

Fig. 42

Fig. 58

Fig. 57

LIGURIANS

One remaining culture which shared with those already described the rite of inhumation burial was that of the Ligurians. Their territory, sandwiched between the Apennines and the Gulf of Genoa, seems to have been another backwater, retaining a primitive culture and a nonIndoEuropean language until a very late date.

Settlements and burials of this people are alike unknown in Tuscany, but the statuemenhirs of the Lunigiana district (see p. 98) are largely concentrated on the east bank of the Magra and so within both Ligurian territory and our area. Though there are reasons for supposing some of them, the Pontevecchio group, to go back to the Copper Age, the Filetto group is certainly Iron Age. These are more elaborate, the head, shoulders and waist often being clearly apparent in the outline of the stone. Face, arms and legs are shown in relief in some detail. Finally, the figure is given weapons which, by including an antenna sword, two or three square spadeshaped axes and

Fig. 30

in many instances lances, remove all doubt as to the date of the statues.

Their function is less obvious. No funerary or other deposit has ever been found with one; at the same time an alternative explanation does not readily offer itself. They may perhaps be memorials set up elsewhere than on the grave. All are clearly male. Carved stelae with some similarities come from the Arnoaldi and Certosa cemeteries in late Villanovan and Etruscan Bologna, and these certainly stood over tombs. A distribution identical with that of the Copper Age menhirs can hardly be a coincidence. It is difficult to bridge the gap in time between the two groups unless we assume that the earlier ones continued to be erected over an enormously long period. More likely is it that, after a long interval, they were still visible and were copied, possibly for a quite different purpose.

CREMATING CULTURES

The Latian Iron Age has been well described in a previous volume in this series, in both its funerary and domestic aspects. But it cannot be completely ignored here without leaving an awkward gap. Its importance lay not in its content but in its future, not in what it was but in what it was to become, the civilisation of Rome. What most needs emphasising is that culturally there was nothing in it to mark it out for future greatness. Any impartial punter would have backed the Villanovans every time. It shows even better than the others what one might call the common denominator of the peninsular Iron Age and this, its native doggedness and its geographical advantages may help to explain why it eventually took the lead in Italy and, later, in the Mediterranaean.

This is not to imply that its material is indistinguishable from that of other contemporary cultures. One pottery vessel at least is characteristic of this group and here very common. It is a

LATIANS

Plate 74

small jar with a reticulate pattern of cordons reminding one of the cane round a ginger jar. Another, the hut-urn, is even more interesting for the light it sheds on the dwellings of the period. Latian bronzes are less distinctive and fewer. The main centres of production were clearly higher up the peninsula, nearer the metal ores.

Plate 73

The hut-urns serve as a good introduction to both the settle-ments and the cemeteries of the Latians. They are terracotta models of dwellings to hold the cremated bones and probably the spirit of the dead. Modest oval or subrectangular buildings are shown, with pitched roofs of which the rafters often project at the ridge. The roof overhangs as eaves on all sides, especially over the doorway where it may form a porch supported on pillars. The square or rounded door is secured by a cross bar. The decoration appearing on some of them is so like that on the Villanovan urns that it is best attributed to the pottery tradition rather than to ornamentation of the huts as such.

That these models are accurate representations of actual huts, possibly even being considered the dwellings of the dead, is confirmed by the excavation of just such huts on the Palatine in Rome. Naturally the wattle-and-daub walls and thatched roofs have long since disappeared, but the plan of the beaten earth floors and the pattern of the post-holes support every detail of the urns where the two can be checked against each other. Consequently the urns can be accepted as evidence for those details of roof construction which the excavations cannot supply. With the help of both, it is not difficult to picture the simple village that was the first Rome of which we have any record.

It stood on the level summit of the Palatine overlooking the cultivated fields of what was to become the Forum, with other hills to the south and east where cattle, sheep and pigs could find grazing. It commanded also the crossing of the River Tiber, the first point above its mouth where the marshy valley floor gave way to firm ground on both banks. From an early date a bridge stood here – it was already old when Horatio held it against the Etruscans. And long before any bridge was built trade was channelled to this point by the topography. Amongst the inhabitants of the Palatine in the eighth century there must already have been traders and craftsmen as well as farmers.

On the valley floor to the north was laid out the cemetery of this village. Though largely disturbed by the great buildings of the Roman Forum, as the village was by the imperial palaces on the Palatine, many graves of the same early date have been discovered. The hut-urns containing the burnt ashes of the dead were placed with other vessels, personal possessions and offerings in large jars in deep pit graves. Many of the burials, however, were inhumations, still with accompanying grave goods, lying in trench graves. The impression is one of a simple people with a modest standard of living and no great social differences.

Plate 74

Many other comparable cemeteries have been found in the hills from Rome south to Terracina, particularly on the fertile slopes of the Alban Mountains. But compared with the other peoples of the Italian Iron Age, the Latians were a small, almost insignificant group, sandwiched between the growing powers of the Etruscans to the north and of the Greek colonies to the south. Rome was to rise from its humble origins higher than either, by the conquest of both.

Looking backward instead of forward for a moment, we can trace the Latian Culture directly back to its origin in the local Final Bronze Age, as shown by the urnfield of Allumiere. No immigration of new people is needed to explain its appearance. The story of Aeneas leading a band of Trojan refugees to found a new home in Latium must be regretfully dismissed as the literary fiction it is.

The Villanovans were the most advanced of the Italian Iron Age peoples, as is shown by the very rich material recovered from their many cemeteries. Yet they still present many unsolved

VILLA-
NOVANS

169

problems. For example, it is only recently that discovery and study of their settlement sites have begun to supplement the funerary evidence, which still provides by far the greater part of our knowledge. Occupation material was found beneath the Etruscan walls of Veii, on the already ancient site of Luni near Civitavecchia and at San Giovenale near by. Several huts of this period were investigated when they came to light in the making of a pedestrian subway in the centre of Bologna. Hut-urns similar to those of the Latians are also known. Even where extensive cemeteries have been found, however, as at Veii and Bologna, they represent not cities but scattered groups of villages made up of such huts. Civilisation in the strict sense began in Italy only with the Greeks and Etruscans.

This intermediate stage of grouped villages, or fragmented towns, was evolved to solve the specific problem raised by the economic bases of Villanovan life. On the one hand a simple farming economy demanded small communities with plenty of accessible agricultural land; on the other, the developing metal industry, not yet advanced enough to rely solely on trade for its food supplies, needed the advantages of a much larger com-munity to allow of craft specialisation. The villages had to have both their fields and each other in order to prosper.

If agriculture was still absolutely necessary to the Villano-vans, what set them in advance of their neighbours was their industries and trade. Both clearly relied on the metal ores of southern Tuscany, including by now exploitation of the rich iron deposits which also occur there. Bronze, though no longer needed in such quantities for tools and weapons, was diverted to the production of those objects for which it remained superior to iron, objects of adornment like fibulae and pendants and the wide range of shapes made possible by the introduction of the techniques of sheet metal working.

This change in the bronze industry is illuminated by a num-ber of hoards distributed through Central Italy. They are often much larger than those of the Bronze Age. One discovered near the church of San Francesco in Bologna in the last century contained very nearly a ton and a half of bronze. They are also quite different in character. Most are certainly and all probably founders' hoards, collections of old worn-out, mis-cast or broken tools, or those rendered obsolete by the introduction of iron. They had no value other than as scrap metal, and were often chopped into shapeless lumps for melting down and recasting. The San Francesco hoard must have been scrap accumulated at a workshop and for some reason never re-worked. Certain hoards, like the famous one from the shore of the picturesque lake of Piediluco, in Umbrian territory near Terni, were more likely loads of metal on their way back to the industrial centres.

One might expect them, then, not only in the region of ex-ploitation of the ores but throughout the area to which bronze was traded in sufficient quantity to make a scrap metal trade profitable. They are in fact no commoner in southern than in northern Tuscany, or in Emilia, the Marche, Umbria or north-ern Latium. It can be no coincidence that the metal ores of Monte Amiata and the Colline Metallifere lie at the very centre of this area.

To see the products of this rich metal industry at their best, one has to turn to the cemeteries. From their beginnings in the mid ninth century at least down to the middle of the eighth, the usual burial rite was inurned cremation. Later, this gradually gave way to trench inhumation. The grave was normally a pit or *pozzetto,* at first circular in shape, later rectangular. Some-times it was lined at the bottom with stone walling or held a stone ossuary. In it stood a tall storeyed urn, a jar with a shoul-der, a long convex neck and a long out-turned lip. There may have been one or two horizontal handles on the shoulder, but if two, the second had been knocked off before burial. The urn contained the cremated bones and ashes of the dead person and usually a few of his or her personal possessions, weapons,

Plate 76

fibulae, spindle whorls or bobbins. Other grave goods were placed around the urn. Apart from nondescript small jars and cups the emphasis seems to have been on ritual rather than func/ tional vessels: offering stands, elaborate rhytons for pouring lib/ ations, small 'incense' burners. The urn had a lid, most often an in/curved lip bowl differing only in detail – decoration, out/ turned base, knobs on the rim – from the standard Pianello one. The occasional hut/urns, already mentioned for the Latians, had of course their own fixed roof/lids, the ashes being inserted through the door in one side.

Plate 72

Plate 73

More interesting is the use of a bronze helmet, or more com/ monly a pottery imitation, to serve as a lid. Two types are found, one having a pointed top and ogival crest, the other a hemispherical skull cap with attachment for a central plume. One of the latter variety from Fermo has, oddly enough, repre/ sentations of the former in its decoration. The helmets are nearly always decorated with embossed circles. Apart from the Coste del Marano cups (see p. 139), they are the first mani/ festation of sheet metal working, which rapidly becomes much commoner and more elaborate. If metal helmets were soon copied in pottery, in the north at least it was not long before pottery urns and table offering stands were copied in metal. As the craftsmen gained confidence in beating and riveting bronze into vessels, so they became more ambitious in the shapes they produced.

Plate 76

Plate 78

Plate 79

The pottery helmets could also be decorated, naturally in techniques more appropriate to their material. The urns them/ selves even more frequently bear ornament. The potters employ/ ed at least five techniques: bands of incised parallel lines (in earlier examples the filling takes the form of diagonal hatching in alternate directions, making in effect hatched triangles), im/ pressed dimples, cord impressions, a sort of incrusted paint and inset of metal studs. Despite this variety, designs are few: a ram/ ifying Z on its side, a swastika, a square frame attached to an outer one by a diagonal line of dots at each corner, a square meander with one or more steps in it. All these techniques and motifs can occur together as on a single urn and helmet-lid from Tarquinia, which lacks only the meander.

Evidence for warfare is present in these cemeteries but rarely obtrusive. The helmets already described are perhaps the most noticeable. Weapons occasionally accompanied the men into their tombs. Spear- or lance-heads differ little from Bronze Age forms, nor does the change from bronze to iron affect their shape much. The short and broad stabbing swords of the period have altered rather more, the wide T-shaped or crescentic pommel becoming characteristic. These again were soon closely copied in iron. Bronze arrowheads appear more rarely, showing that the bow was in use also. Perhaps the horse, now becoming much commoner, should also be classed as a weapon of war since this was undoubtedly its prime function. Elaborate bronze bits and cheek-pieces were included in the dead man's equipment so that he could command the use of horses in the next world as in this. Warriors on horseback are frequent motifs on the later grave stelae of Bologna. Bits found in pairs on the other hand seem to suggest the continuing use of the chariot.

It would be a mistake to over-emphasise the warlike nature of the Villanovans. With mankind warfare is so universal and, even more oddly, so glorified that it is the absence rather than the presence of evidence for it which calls for special comment. Here it should be remembered that graves without weapons greatly outnumber those having them. And although many Villanovan settlement sites were chosen for their natural defences (Luni offering a good example), this was not always an over-riding factor. Bologna lay in near-level country although steep hills were at hand immediately to the south. It was sited for its strategic position not for war but for trade and industry, the true mainsprings of Villanovan life.

Plate 76

Fig. 42

Fig. 60

Fig. 59

The industry in question was actively developing. The more important broad changes have been already referred to: the re-placement of bronze by iron for functional tools and weapons, the great increase in decorative bronze work made possible in consequence, and the appearance and elaboration of sheet metal work. For elucidating the history of particular groups of ceme-teries, it is the smaller and subtler changes in particular metal

Fig. 42

types that are the more useful. Though weapons altered little, axes were made in several successive forms. On the winged axe, the wings were moved up to the butt, making the so-called end-winged axe. Later the blade was widened into what is known as the spade-shaped axe, which was in turn largely replaced by the shaft-hole form in iron. The quadrangular razors popular in the Pianello urnfields were early replaced by broad crescentic forms. Later they disappeared altogether, either because the wavy knives were being used in their stead or per-haps because beards came back into fashion.

Most important of all is the long and at first glance very tang-

Fig. 57

led history of the fibula. When understood, however, it is one of the best known examples of a typological series, a slow development by means of small and cumulative changes com-parable to the evolution of a natural species propounded by Charles Darwin or the history of the rifle discussed by General Pitt-Rivers. The fibulae vary by virtue of changes brought about solely by the vagaries of fashion or the whim of the crafts-men; a sixth-century fibula is functionally neither better nor worse at its job than one of the twelfth century, great though the difference between them may be.

The bronze fibula, like its modern counterpart the safety pin, consists basically of four parts: a sharp pin to hold the cloth, a spring to allow it freedom of movement, a catchplate to receive the point of the pin and a bow to hold the catchplate and pin in the correct relative positions. Most variation is found in the bow. Two major lines of development can be traced, with

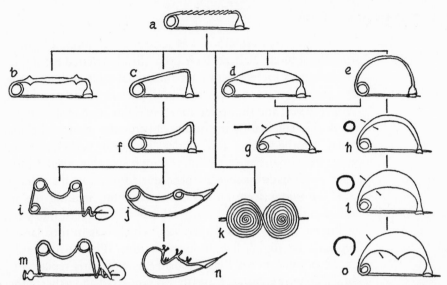

Fig. 57. The development of the fibula in Italy. Late Bronze Age: a, Violin bow (ad arco di violino). *Final Bronze Age: b, knobbed violin bow; c, elbowed* (a staffa lunga); *d, foliate* (a foglia); *e, arc* (ad arco semplice). *Iron Age: f, stilted* (a gomito); *g, willow leaf; h, leech* (a sanguisuga); *i, Terni, with disc catchplate; j, serpent* (serpeggiante); *k, spectacle; l, swollen bow; m, separate pin; n, dragon* (a drago); *o, boat* (a navicella).

concave and convex bows respectively. Both start from the straight-backed violin-bow fibula of the Late Bronze Age, the former progressing through the elbowed fibula already met with and the stilted form, *a gomito,* where the concave back first appears. The pin is soon given a corresponding curve. Progressive exaggeration leads to the serpent-like and dragon fibulae, *serpeggiante* and *a drago,* in ever more baroque forms.

The convex bow fibulae on the other hand descend from the arc fibula, which derived from the violin-bow form before it reached Italy. Here the tendency is towards thickening rather than curvature of the bow: the swollen bow or leech fibula, *a sanguisuga,* and the boat-shaped fibula, *a navicella,* in which the bow is larger still but hollow and open in the inside of the curve.

The names are usually well chosen to describe the shape. In many the thickening is not in the bronze of the bow itself but is produced by threading on it blocks of amber, ivory or even transverse discs of bronze to give the swelling outline.

Two types of fibulae are distinguished by having different forms of catchplate, their bows being as variable as those with the normal plate. Early in the Iron Age a form was current in which the catch opened into a large flat spiral, the disc-plate fibula. Later a much longer catchplate became almost universal, and when terminated with a knob is known as the Certosa fibula, after the Etruscan cemetery at Bologna. It is this which was ancestral to the La Tène fibulae of continental Europe. There are other side-branches of development which can be more or less easily related to one of the two main ones, but the spectacle fibula represents an unrelated type introduced from the Balkans, where it had developed independently out of the violin-bow form.

Using the changing fibulae to give a relative time-scale, two groups of cemeteries will be described in some detail to illustrate the history of Villanovan development in the two main areas of its distribution.

The oldest cemetery at Tarquinia in the south is that of Sel-ciatello, lying nearest the ancient city. Its early date is shown by the fact that a third of the razors found there were of the quadran-gular variety current at Pianello. The characteristic fibula had a disc catchplate. Although no sheet metal was found, pottery imitations of bronze helmets show that it was already being produced. As the available burial space was used up, new cemeteries were started progressively further afield. In that on the Poggio del Impicato, the razors were all of the full Villanov-

Fig. 58

Plate 76

an crescentic form and the first leech fibulae had appeared. At Sopra-Selciatello and Monterozzi the commonest fibula was that in which the bow is swollen to a boat shape, often pinched into a lozenge rather than the simple bloated convex form. In one grave was a sword of a type with a pommel composed of two opposed spirals, to which we shall have to return shortly. It is the Hallstatt antenna sword. Other evidence of external contact is given by the appearance among the hand-made, dark polished, local urns of a few red or yellowish wheel-turned, and one or two simple painted, vessels. How many of these, and which, are of Geometric Greek manufacture or at least in-piration is a matter of some controversy. The Villanovan urn itself changes only little, tending to become taller and thinner. The foreign influences strengthen rapidly and all later cemeteries at Tarquinia are Etruscan rather than Villanovan.

Although no discussion of the problem of Etruscan origins can be attempted here, it is worth pointing out that the two main theories are no longer contradictory. Those scholars who favour an immigration from Asia Minor now realise that the Etruscans in the strict sense, wherever they came from, were a small minority and the Villanovans formed the bulk of the population. The origin of the latter will occupy our attention in a moment. On the other hand, however strong the local element, much Etruscan material is unarguably of oriental character. Now that the revised dating of the earliest Greek and Etruscan material puts them so close together in time, it is be-coming more and more difficult to decide if any one article or trait came by way of Greek commerce or as Etruscan hand-luggage. It can be seen, therefore, that both Italy and the Aeg-ean played a large part in forming the Etruscan civilisation; exactly how great was the contribution of each may never be finally settled.

The Villanovans themselves appear to have a similar dual origin. The old view that they represent a wholesale immigration from beyond the Alps is no longer tenable. If one looks outside Italy, there is nothing more obviously 'proto⁄Villano⁄ van' than was already present within the peninsula at the urn⁄ fields of Allumiere or even Pianello itself. To mention a few raits only, cremation, *pozzetto* urnfields, stones to mark the tombs, pottery urns, the bowl lids, groove and dimple decor⁄ ation, the meander, the double⁄sling motif, arc fibulae, all in⁄ dividually provide more or less convincing links and together they become even more impressive. On the other hand iron can hardly be a local invention. It implies newcomers, if only a few influential craftsmen, from the east. Other traits like the horse⁄bits, the hut⁄urns and in all probability the important technique of sheet metal work, point almost as clearly to influ⁄ ence from beyond the Alps. But we have no means of telling how many men came with them.

The relationship between the two main areas of distribution of the Villanovans, Tuscany⁄Latium (with widespread outliers like Fermo in the Marche and Pontecagnano near Salerno) and Emilia, also remains obscure. The great Iron Age centre of Bologna sprang up at a major route junction. Southwards, passes crossed the Apennines to Etruria. East and west ran the age⁄old track along the edge of the Po marshes. Beyond these to the north lay the valley of the Adige leading directly to the Brenner Pass and the whole of Central Europe. Its immensely wealthy cemeteries have been exhaustively studied in the centu⁄ ry since 1859 when the first of them was discovered at Villanova itself, a hamlet four miles east of the city.

Since the contents of the earliest of these cemeteries, outside the Porta San Vitale and at San Lazzaro di Savena, look sim⁄ pler but slightly later than the earliest at Tarquinia or Veii, the tendency recently has been to regard the northern branch as the offshoot of the southern. Though proof is still lacking, this does seem likely, the settlement being explained as first a trading post, then a manufacturing centre, on the route towards the

Plate 78, 79

Fig. 59

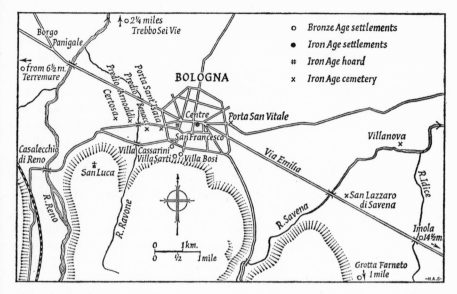

Fig. 59. Sites in the Bologna district

rich markets of the continent. Only one razor of the quadran-
gular form was found and among the fibulae were leech types   Fig. 57
which had already lost the early disc-shaped catchplate. One
horse-bit appeared and there were several records of sheet bronze
work. These cemeteries probably go back to around 800 BC.

The next cemeteries were those at the Porta Sant'Isaia and
on the Benacci estate. The disc-plate fibulae had gone out of
favour, the leech and boat forms becoming the most popular.
Spade-shaped axes were now frequent but weapons rare. Bits   Fig. 42
were much commoner, including ones with cheek-pieces in
the shape of stylised horses. The greatest advance had been   Fig. 60
made in sheet metal work, particularly bronze copies of the
urns and the first broad and highly ornamented belts. It was   cf. Plate 80
at the end of this period that the Etruscans appeared in the
south, but Bologna was left undisturbed for another century
or more allowing the Villanovan craftsmen to reach even higher
peaks of achievement.

The Sant'Isaia cemetery continued and a new one came into use further out in the Benacci property, known simply as Benacci II. The most noticeable feature here was the great increase in wealth. Iron was now in common use. Sheet bronze was not only more frequent but much more elaborate – buckets, urns, pedestalled and cupped offering tables, belts. Solid bronze by no means disappeared, there being crescentic razors, wavy-bladed knives, spade-shaped axes now so light as to be of more use as knives, swords derived from the spiral-hilted ones, bits, pins, rings, armlets and other ornaments. Boat fibulae were by this time common and the tendency towards a long catchplate was becoming apparent. The first painted pottery vessels show that influence from the south was beginning to make itself felt.

Next again was the still richer Arnoaldi cemetery. Here the Villanovan urn had altered almost out of recognition, its decoration being entirely by the new technique of stamp impressions. All fibulae now had the long catchplates, and razors suddenly disappeared. The Certosa cemetery of the sixth century can be regarded as fully Etruscanised; the Villanovan Culture had been absorbed by its more powerful successor after three centuries of brilliant development.

The importance of the Villanovans is threefold. The products of their craftsmanship speak to us directly across the centuries, particularly the engraved metalwork. The bronze belts, helmets and embossed buckets are masterpieces by any standards. Secondly, they played a crucial part in the formation of the Etruscan civilisation, and through it that of Rome. Their influence on later history in Northern Italy was less marked by reason of the incursion of the Gallic tribes in the fourth century. Thirdly, just as they acquired the knowledge of iron by way of the sea routes from the Aegean, so they passed it on by the land routes, along with many of their bronze products, to the northern slopes of the Alps. There it provided one of the main incentives to the rise of the equally brilliant Hallstatt Culture

Plate 80

Fig. 58

Plate 81

Plates 78, 79, 80

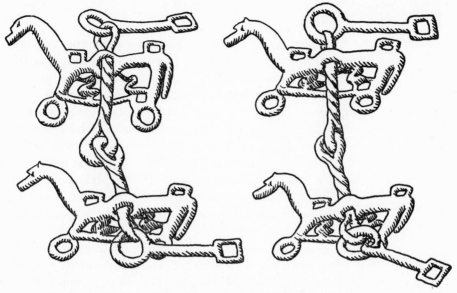

Fig. 60. Pair of horse bits from a tomb in the Benacci cemetery, Bologna

which opened the Trans-Alpine Iron Age. Trade and influence were not in one direction only. If the Italian sword
appears occasionally in Central Europe, so does the Hallstatt
antenna sword in Italy. If the Villanovan double sling, ultimately derived from Pianello, was enthusiastically adopted
across the Alps, so was the Hallstatt duck motif in exchange.
The widespread bird, boat and sun-disc motif was a hybrid
between the two. And as the first objects of iron were carried
northward over the Brenner they passed amber being traded
southwards in greater quantity than ever before.

Plate 80
Plate 64

CHAPTER VII

Postscript

THE TIME HAS COME to recapitulate briefly the conclusions reached. Interesting though the trees are, the wood is
the main object of study, and a very hoary and tangled wood it
seems to be.

The scarcity of material surviving from the immensely long
Palaeolithic period suggests that the hunting population must
have been very small at the time of the first arrival of the Neolithic farmers. Even so, we saw reason to think that there was
some contact between them, which may have included inter-
marrying. How far population growth through the succeeding
centuries was due to natural increase in a virgin land and how
far to reinforcement by sea it is so far very difficult to say. The
long periods of time known to be involved, together with the
improvements in food production, argue one way, the scarcity
of early sites the other. Clearly both must have played their part.

The Copper Age opens with new peoples moving into the
peninsula, probably by sea. The appearance of a substantial
proportion of round heads amongst the skulls of the time is
conclusive. Some cultural changes, however, may be explained
in other ways, by war and trade, but as we saw, large parts of
the centre and east remained unaffected.

Ethnically and culturally the peninsular Bronze Age opens
with a period of fusion between the earlier elements without
further immigration. Later there are three exceptions. The cos-
mopolitan character of Taranto could well have attracted foreign traders to settle, but their numbers are unlikely to have
been very great. The close contact between Dalmatia and the
Grotta Manaccora in the Final Bronze Age could imply settlers
from beyond the Adriatic joining the native inhabitants at that
one site. Much more important, in the north the Terramara

Culture looks very foreign in every respect and can only be explained by a considerable movement of population from the Danube valley.

It is not until these elements become fully assimilated in the Final Bronze Age that we can first feel reasonably sure that we may speak of *Italici,* if we want to. If invasion is necessary to introduce a new language, Indo-European probably entered Italy with the *terramaricoli.* However, language, material culture, race, religion and burial rite can each on occasion travel completely independently of any or all of the others. It is dangerous to try to take such intangible things as the names of peoples or spoken languages any further back than the only possible evidence for them, namely writing, will permit.

By the Iron Age the uniformity was giving way and local groups had appeared in the peninsula to which we can begin to apply recorded names, such as Latins, Picenes, Daunians, with rather more confidence. In Apulia there is surviving cultural influence from Mycenaean Greece. The Villanovans were in fairly close contact with Central Europe at all stages, and the eastern coast of Italy with Dalmatia. Otherwise there is no need to call in further immigration until the beginning of the Greek colonisation, the Etruscans if they were truly foreign, and rather later the Gauls. But all these are, if not in historic times, at least on the verge of them. In 753 BC, according to tradition, was founded the city and power of Rome, an explosive mixture of Greek sulphur, Etruscan saltpetre and charcoal from that ancient wood of prehistoric Italy.

Select Bibliography

Abbreviations

Antiq.	*Antiquity*
A.A.E.	*Archivio per Antropologia ed Etnologia*
A.I.C.	*Atti del 1° Congresso Internazionale di Preistoria e Protostoria Mediterranea 1950*
B.P.I.	*Bullettino di Paletnologia Italiana*
Mon. Ant.	*Monumenti Antichi*
Not.Sc.	*Notizie degli Scavi*
P.B.S.R.	*Papers of the British School at Rome*
P.P.S.	*Proceedings of the Prehistoric Society*
Riv. Antr.	*Rivista di Antropologia*
R.S.P.	*Rivista di Scienze Preistoriche*
St. Etr.	*Studi Etruschi*

General Works

BERNABÒ BREA, L., *Gli scavi nella Caverna delle Arene Candide*, II. Bordighera, 1956
—, *Sicily*. London, 1957
CIANFARANI, V., *et al.*, *Trecentomila anni di vita in Abruzzo*. Chieti, 1962
DUHN, F. VON, *Italische Gräberkunde*. Heidelberg, 1924, 1939
GUIDO, M., *Sardinia*. London, 1963
MONTELIUS, O., *La civilisation primitive en Italie*. Stockholm, 1895–1910
—, *Die Vorklassische Chronologie Italiens*. Stockholm, 1912
PATRONI, G., *La Preistoria*. Rome, 1935
PEET, T. E., *The Stone and Bronze Ages in Italy*. Oxford, 1909
PITTIONI, R., *Italien, Urgeschichtliche Kulturen*. Stuttgart, 1962
RADMILLI, A. M. (ed.), *Piccola Guida della Preistoria Italiana*. Florence, 1962
—, *La Preistoria d'Italia alla luce delle ultime scoperte*. Florence, 1963
TOURING CLUB ITALIANO, *L'Italia Fisica*. Milan, 1957

Central and Southern Italy

Palaeolithic

BLANC, A. C., Giacimento ed industria del paleolitico inferiore e fauna fossile ad Elephas a Torre in Pietra presso Roma. *Riv. Antr.* XLI, 1954

—, Sulle veneri del Trasimeno e di Willendorf. *Quaternaria* I, 1954

—, Torre in Pietra, Saccopastore e Monte Circeo. *Bollettino della Società Geografica Italiana,* 1958

—, *et al.* Excursions dans les Abruzzes, les Pouilles et sur la côte de Salerno. *Inqua,* Rome and Pisa, 1953

BLANC, G. A., Grotta Romanelli. *A.A.E.* L, 1920; LVIII, 1928

GRAZIOSI, P., *L'arte dell'antica età della pietra.* Florence, 1956

RADMILLI, A. M., Insediamenti preistorici in Abruzzo. *L'Universo,* XXXIX, 1959

TONGIORGI, E., and A. M. RADMILLI, Gli scavi nella Grotta La Porta di Positano. Contributo alla conoscenza del mesolitico italiano. *R.S.P.* XIII, 1958, p. 91

ZORZI, F., Palaeolithic discoveries in the Grotta Paglicci. *Antiq.* XXXVIII, 1964, no. 149, p. 38

Neolithic

BRADFORD, J., and P. R. WILLIAMS-HUNT, Siticulosa Apulia. *Antiq.* XX, 1946, no. 80, p. 191

—, The Apulia Expedition, an interim report. *Antiq.* XXIV, 1950, no. 94, p. 84

BUCHNER, G., La stratigrafia dei livelli a ceramica ed i ciottoli dipinti schematici antropomorfi della Grotta delle Felci. *B.P.I.* n.s. IX, 1954–55, p. 107

CIANFARANI, V., *et al., Op. cit.*

CORNAGGIA CASTIGLIONI, O., and L. MENGHI, La Grotta delle Mura – Monopoli. *B.P.I.* n.s. XI, 1957, p. 56

MAYER, M., *Le stazioni preistoriche di Molfetta.* Bari, 1904

—, *Molfetta und Matera.* Leipzig, 1924

MOSSO, A., La necropoli neolitica di Molfetta. *Mon. Ant.* XX, 1910, col. 237

PATRIZI, S., *et al.,* Sepoltura ad inumazione con cranio trapanato della Grotta Patrizi, Sasso-Furbara. *Riv. Antr.* XLI, 1954, p. 33

PUGLISI, S. M., Industria microlitica nei livelli a ceramica impressa di Coppa Nevigata. *R.S.P.* X, 1955, p. 19

—, Nota preliminare sugli scavi nella Caverna dell'Erba (Avetrana). *R.S.P.* VIII, 1953, p. 86

QUAGLIATI, Q., *La Puglia Preistorica.* Trani, 1936

RELLINI, U., *La più antica ceramica dipinta in Italia.* Rome, 1934

—, La Grotta delle Felci a Capri. *Mon. Ant.* XXIX, 1923, col. 305

RIDOLA, D., Le grande trincee preistoriche di Matera. *B.P.I.* XLIV, 1924, p. 97; XLV, 1925, p. 85; XLVI, 1926, p. 134

STEVENSON, R. B. K., Neolithic Cultures of South-east Italy. *P.P.S.* 1947, p. 85

TRUMP, D.H., The prehistoric settlement at La Starza, Ariano Irpino. *P.B.S.R.* XXV, 1957, p. 1

—, Excavation at La Starza, Ariano Irpino. *P.B.S.R.* XXXI, 1963, p. 1

Copper Age

ACANFORA, M.O., Fontanella Mantovano e la cultura di Remedello. *B.P.I.* n.s. X, 1956, p. 321

—, Le stele antropomorfe di Castelluccio dei Sauri. *R.S.P.* XV, 1960, p. 95

BIANCOFIORE, F., Tomba di tipo siculo con nuovo osso a globuli nel territorio di Altamura, Bari. *B.P.I.* n.s. XI, 1957, p. 153

CAMBIO, L., I metalli dei cimeli della grotta tombale di Monte Bradoni (Volterra). *B.P.I.* n.s. XII, 1958, p. 137

COLINI, G. A., Il sepolcreto di Remedello Sotto nel Bresciano e il periodo eneolitico in Italia. *B.P.I.* XXIV–XXVIII, 1898–1901 (12 parts)

FORMENTINI, U., Statue stele della Lunigiana. *St. Etr.* I, 1927, p. 61

GRAZIOSI, P., Resti umani della necropoli preistorica di Paestum. *R.S.P.* II, 1947, p. 290

—, Resti umani della necropoli preistorica di Ischia di Castro (Viterbo). *R.S.P.* III, 1948, p. 113

LO PORTO, F.G. La tomba di Cellino San Marco e l'inizio della civiltà del bronzo in Puglia. *B.P.I.* n.s. XIV, 1962–63, p. 191

PALUMBO, G., Inventario delle pietre fitte salentine. *R.S.P.* X, 1955, p. 86

—, Inventario dei dolmen di Terra d'Otranto. *R.S.P.* XI, 1956, p. 84

RITTATORE, F., Scoperte di età eneolitica e del bronze nella Maremma Tosco-Laziale. *R.S.P.* VI, 1951, p. 3

SESTIERI, P.C., La necropoli preistorica di Paestum. *R.S.P.* I, 1946, p. 245; II, 1947, p. 283; and *A.I.C.* p. 195

TRUMP, D.H., *Op. cit.*

Bronze Age

BAUMGÄRTEL, E., The cave of Manaccora, Monte Gargano. *P.B.S.R.* XIX, 1951, p. 25; XXI, 1953, p. 1

BUCHNER, G., Nota preliminare sulle ricerche preistoriche nell'isola d'Ischia. *B.P.I.* n.s. I, 1936–37, p. 65

CALZONI, U., Topografia e scavi nelle stazioni preistoriche della Montagna di Cetona (Belverde). *Quaderni dell'Istituto di St. Etr.* I, 1954; II, 1962

COLINI, G.A., La civiltà del bronzo in Italia. *B.P.I.* XXIX, 1903, p. 53, 211

—, Necropoli di Pianello di Genga (Arcevia) e l'origine della civiltà del ferro in Italia. *B.P.I.* XXXIX, 1913, p. 19; XL, 1914, p. 121; XLI, 1915, p. 128

GERVASIO, M., *I dolmen e la civiltà del bronzo nelle Puglie.* Bari, 1913

HAWKES, C.F.C., Chronology of the Bronze and Early Iron Ages, Greek, Italian and Trans-Alpine. *A.I.C.* p. 256

LOLLINI, D., *et al.*, Ricerche intorno la Gola del Sentino. *B.P.I.* n.s. X, 1956, p. 491

MANSUELLI, G.A., and R.SCARANI, *Emilia prima dei Romani.* Milan, 1961

MOSSO, A., Stazione preistorica di Coppa Nevigata, Manfredonia. *Mon. Ant.* XIX, 1908, col. 305

PATRONI, G., Caverna naturale con avanzi preistorici in provincia di Salerno (Pertosa). *Mon. Ant.* IX, 1899, col. 545

PERONI, R., Per una definizione dell'aspetto culturale subapenninico. *Atti dell'Accademia Nazionale dei Lincei (Sc. mor., stor. e fil.)* ser. VIII, vol. IX, 1959, p. 3

PUGLISI, S.M., *La civiltà apenninica.* Florence, 1959

QUAGLIATI, Q., Abitato terramaricolo, Scoglio del Tonno, Taranto. *Not. Sc.* 1900, p. 411

RELLINI, U., Caverna di Latronico. *Mon. Ant.* XXIV, 1916, col. 461
—, Le stazioni enee delle Marche di fase seriore e la civiltà italica. *Mon. Ant.* XXXIV, 1932, col. 129
—, La civiltà enea in Italia. *B.P.I.* LIII, 1933, p. 63; LIV, 1934, p. 65
SÄFLUND, G., Le terremare delle provincie di Modena, Reggio Emilia, Parma, Piacenza. *Acta Instituti Romani Regni Sueciae*, VII, 1939
TAYLOUR, LORD WILLIAM, *Mycenean pottery in Italy.* Cambridge, 1958
—, *The Mycenaeans.* London, 1964
TRUMP, D.H., *Op. cit.*
—, The Apennine Culture of Italy. *P.P.S.* XXIV, 1958, p. 165

Iron Age

ANNIBALDI, G., Rinvenimento a Fermo di tombe a cremazione di tipo villanoviano. *B.P.I.* n.s. X, 1956, p. 229
BLOCH, R., *The Etruscans.* London, 1958
—, *The Origins of Rome.* London, 1960
BRIZIO, E., La necropoli di Novilara. *Mon. Ant.* V, 1895, col. 85
DRAGO, C., Tumuli sepolcrali 'a specchia' della penisola salentina. *Riv. Antr.* XLI, 1954, p. 382
DUNBABIN, T.J., *The Western Greeks.* Oxford, 1948
GABRICI, E., Cumae. *Mon. Ant.* XXII, 1913, col. 5
LEOPOLD, H., Il ripostiglio di Piediluco. *B.P.I.* n.s. III, 1939, p. 143
LOLLINI, D., L'abitato preistorico e protostorico di Ancona. *B.P.I.* n.s. X, 1956, p. 237
MACIVER, D.RANDALL, *Villanovans and Early Etruscans.* Oxford, 1924
—, *The Early Iron Age in Italy.* Oxford, 1927
ORSI, P., Necropoli pre-elleniche calabresi di Torre Galli e di Canale, Janchina, Patariti. *Mon. Ant.* XXXI, 1926, col. 5
PALLOTTINO, M., *The Etruscans.* London, 1955
SESTIERI, P.C., Necropoli villanoviana in provincia di Salerno (Pontecagnano). *St. Etr.* XXVIII, 1960, p. 73
SUNDWALL, J., *Die älteren italischen Fibeln.* Berlin, 1943
WOODHEAD, A.G., *The Greeks in the West.* London, 1962

Sources of Illustrations

Without the co-operation of many Museums, Soprintendenze alle Antichità and other institutions, it would have been impossible to obtain as full a photographic record of the material as appears in the plates. I must thank the following for providing me with photographs: the National Museums of Ancona (Numbers 16, 38, 39, 47, 56, 57, 61, 62, 64, and 77–79), Naples (29–32, 40–42, 49, 50 and 70), Perugia (48, 51, 54, 55 and 65), the Pigorini and Latium Museums at Rome (35, 36, 66, 67, 73 and 74), the Civic Museum at Bologna (60, 80 and 81) and Florence University (68). All other photographs of museum objects are by the author, with the generously accorded permission of their custodians, Rome University, the British School at Rome, the National Museums of Bari, Matera, the Pigorini and, above all, Taranto. I owe Plate 1 to the generosity of Dr D. Adamasteanu of the Aerofototeca, Rome. The other site photographs are my own.

The maps and text figures 8, 29 and 52 were drawn by H. A. Shelley. The other text figures are by the author. Where they are at second hand this is acknowledged in their captions.

THE PLATES

1

2

3

4

5

6

7

11

12

15

16

17

18

19

20

21

22

23

24

25

26

27

28

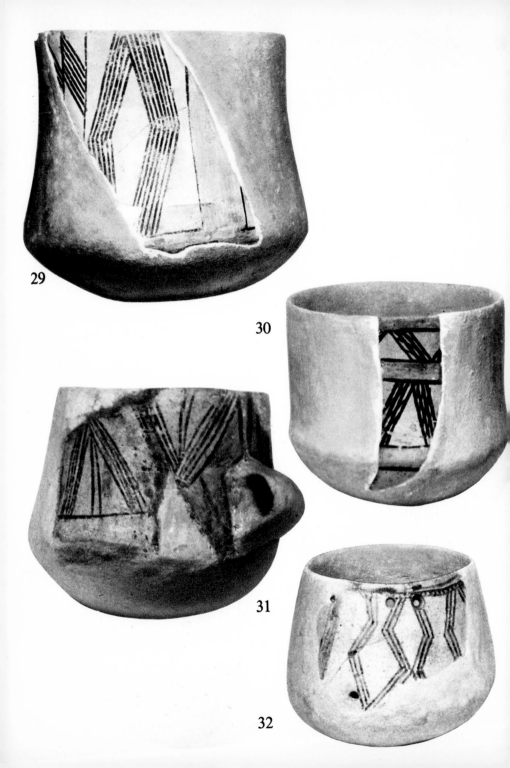

29

30

31

32

33

34

35

36

37

38

39

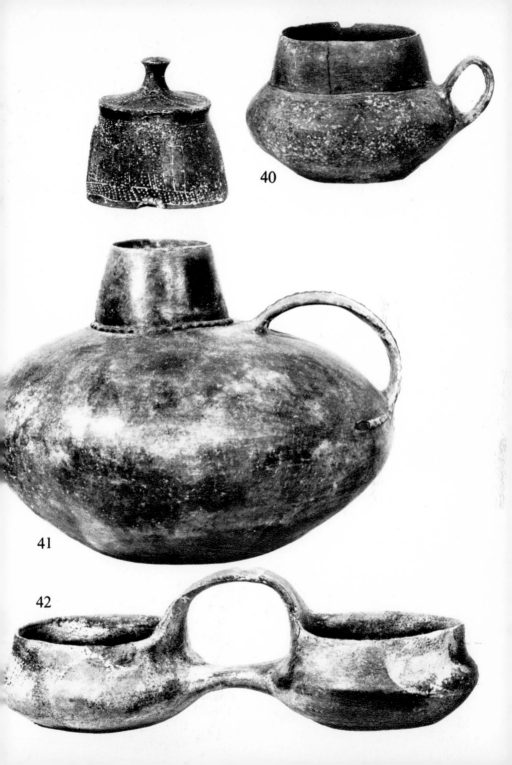

40

41

42

43

44

45

46

47

48

49

50

51

52

53

54

55

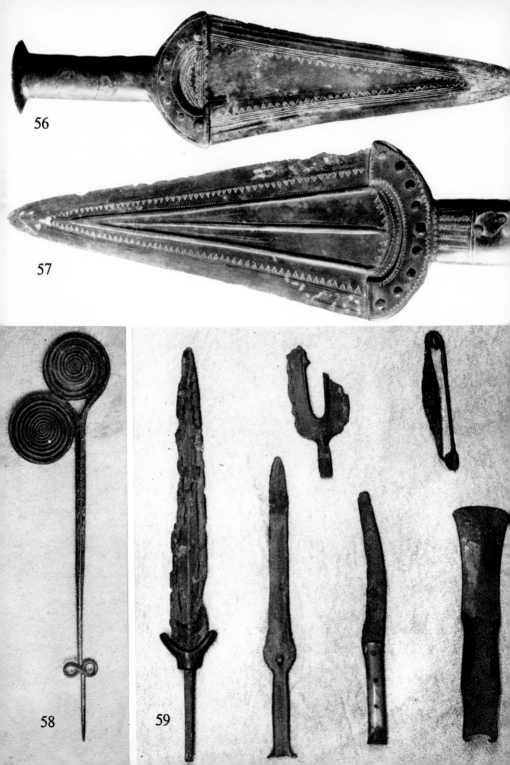

56

57

58

59

60
61

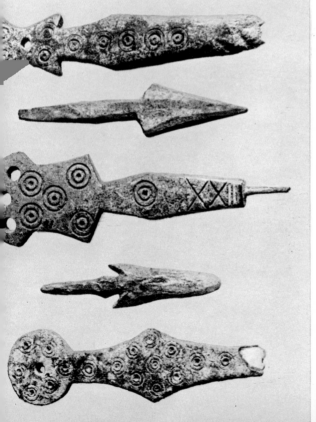

62

63

64

65

66

67

68

69

70

71

72

73

74

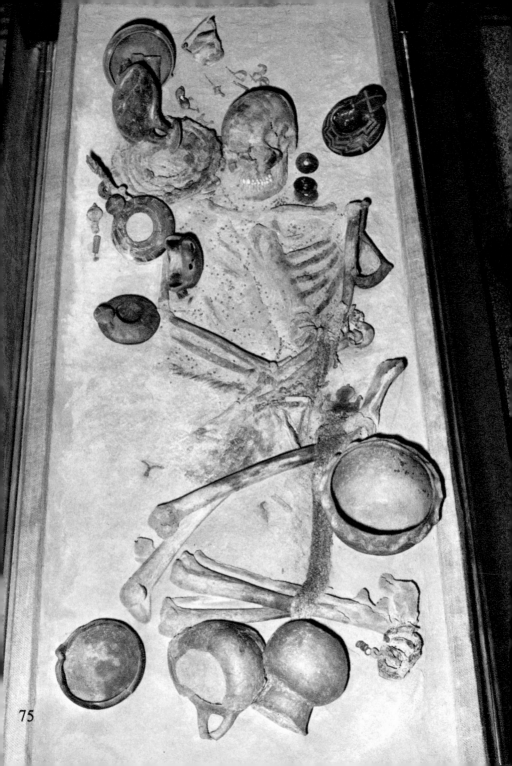

76

77

78

79

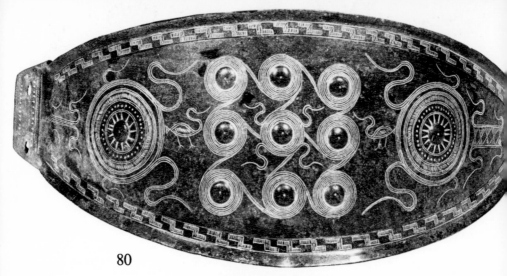

80

81

Notes on the Plates

1 Air photograph of one of the 250 or so Neolithic villages discovered by this means by Bradford in 1943-45 on the Tavoliere, the plain around Foggia. This one lies 4 miles north-east of Lucera. It consists of two pairs of concentric ditches revealed by crop marks. Inside these are a number of smaller ditched enclosures, probably hut compounds, seen most clearly in the upper half of the plate. The huts within these have left only scanty traces which cannot be seen from the air. The straight parallel lines at the bottom are probably a Roman feature. The scale is given by the farms in the upper corners and the sheep at bottom centre.

2 The Pulo di Molfetta, a dolina or collapsed cave in the limestone of the Murge, 15 miles west of Bari. The caves in the hundred-foot cliffs of this circular depression were occupied in the Early Bronze Age. Neolithic huts were found under the olive groves both on its floor and on the level ground above, where there was also a cemetery of crouched burials of the same date. The site has given its name to the Italian version of the Impressed Ware.

3 Panoramic view of the gorge below Matera. The old city lies on the left, dominated by the cathedral. The Neolithic ditched village of La Murgecchia occupies the hilltop between the two branches of the gorge in the centre of the plate, hiding Serra d'Alto 3 miles to the north. To the right is the slope of Murgia Timone, with another ditched Neolithic village and Final Bronze Age rock-cut tombs. The Grotta dei Pipistrelli opens in the wall of the gorge 2 miles downstream behind the camera. Many other caves can be seen in the cliffs, the group in the centre being inhabited until recent times, as some in the lower part of the city are today. See Fig. 9.

4 The gypsum hill of La Starza, Ariano Irpino, Avellino province. This commands the low pass between Campania and Apulia, lying about 2 miles from the watershed. It was occupied from the Early Neolithic to the Early Iron Age. Excavations by the author revealed 20 feet of deposit

covering the Late Neolithic and Copper Ages in the lip of the cliff in the centre of the plate in 1962 and 18 feet of late Copper Age to Iron Age on a terrace on the further, northern side of the hill in 1961.

5 Ponte San Pietro over the River Fiora, Viterbo province, but very close to the borders of Tuscany. A medieval bridge was replaced by the modern one on the left. On the hilltop above it, around the present farm, stood the Final Bronze Age village of Pianizza, the urnfield cemetery of which was found in the field on the valley floor at the bottom of the plate. The Copper Age cemetery of rockcut tombs was excavated in the bank of tuff at the righthand edge of the hill immediately above the road.

6 The Scusi dolmen at Minervino di Lecce, 5 miles southeast of Otranto, probably of the Copper Age. It stands now on bare limestone among olive groves, a slab of rock 12½ feet long supported on roughly built walls. There are close similarities with the dolmens of Malta and Sardinia. Compare with Plate 7. See also Fig. 27.

7 Gallery Grave at Bisceglie, 21 miles west of Bari. One capstone, most of the orthostatic walls and traces of an original cairn mound survive. A plan is given in Fig. 46. It held the remains of eleven skeletons and was dated by the associated finds to the Final Bronze Age.

8 Two of the characteristic monuments of the Apulian Murge, a *specchia* and a *trullo* at Martano, 16 miles southeast of Lecce. The *specchia* is a large cairn of unknown purpose and possible Iron Age date. Smaller examples have been found covering burial cists of that period but excavations on the larger ones such as this have so far been fruitless. The *trullo* is a drystone hut with a corbelled roof. This one is about 10 feet high and used for storing agricultural tools and produce but many a little further north are still used as dwellings. Surviving examples are all recent though their origins must go back to an early if unknown period.

9 A 10 foot menhir standing outside the village of Giurdignano, 3½ miles west of Otranto and 2 from the Minervino dolmen in Plate 6. These strange monuments are thickly scattered through this remote corner of Italy. Their date and function are alike uncertain.

10 Defensive ditch of the Copper Age village of Conelle di Arcevia, 26 miles west of Ancona. It spans the neck of a gravel promontory between two streams. At this point it is a little over 10 feet deep, in other places running even deeper. In it were found large quantities of pottery, arrow, heads and domestic rubbish from the village.

11 General view of Belverde di Cetona near Chiusi. On the top of the travertine cliff is a defensive wall probably of the Iron Age. In the tum, bled rock at its foot, largely masked by trees, are the carved boulders and caves used from the Copper to the Iron Ages for burials and votive depos, its. The material of the Late and Final Bronze Ages was particularly rich, supported by the working of the metal deposits to the west. Lower on the slope was an open village of this same period. Beneath the cypresses to the right is a charming medieval hermitage with beyond it a distant view of the Tuscan countryside. Behind the camera is Casa Carletti, a village of the Final Bronze Age.

12 One of the rock carvings of Belverde, the so,called 'Amphitheatre'. This is misleading as it opens at the front directly onto the slope. The steps were clearly intended for seating for which, apart from their hardness, they are not too uncomfortable. Whether it served for religious, administrative or other gatherings is not known.

13 The Gola del Sentino, Genga, 32 miles south,west of Ancona. The Middle Bronze Age village of Spineto lies out of the plate to the right. The famous urnfield of Pianello covered the flat valley floor at the centre just before it closes into the gorge. The Late Bronze Age cave site of Frasassi is high in the gorge's left,hand wall with an open site of the same date below it. The Final Bronze Age caves of Baffoni and Mezzogiorno, both with a little Neolithic material in their lowest levels, open in the cliffs above the lower mouth of the gorge a little over a mile downstream. See Fig. 45.

14 The Grotta Manaccora on the north coast of the Gargano. The great cave opens directly on the beach. The photograph is taken from the rocky headland which had an open village site of the same Late Bronze to Iron Age date. Inland can be seen the wild country of the Foresta d'Umbra,

227

which makes access by land from Foggia harder than it is by sea from Dalmatia.

15 Sherds of Impressed (Molfetta) Ware showing the different techniques of decoration. The first is impressed with the edge of a cockle shell, the so-called cardial ware, the second with a stick or bone slip, the third is slashed. In the lower row the first two are finger-tipped, one poked and the other pinched, and the third has the characteristic rocker pattern. The length of the longest sherd is 11.3 cms. From the Grotta Scaloria, Manfredonia; now in the Taranto Museum.

16 Jar of Impressed (Ripabianca) Ware from Ripabianca di Monterado, Ancona. The decoration is split up into panels separated by low ribs but the fabric and shape of the pot are little different from the ancestral Molfetta Ware. Height 27 cms. Ancona Museum.

17 Open jar or deep bowl from the Grotta Ostuni, diameter 21.9 cms. The neck, illustrating most of the motifs found on Matera Scratched Ware, is separated by a low cordon from the lower wall, on which are rows of rocker pattern derived from Molfetta Impressed Ware. Its base is missing. Taranto Museum.

18 Flint flakes from the Grotta Scaloria, an undistinguished selection showing an average group of flints from an Apulian Neolithic site. The longest is 10.3 cms. Taranto Museum.

19 By contrast, four long flint blades of exceptional quality from Monteparano near Taranto. The longest is 26.3 cms. Taranto Museum.

20 Fragment of large globular bowl of Red on Buff Painted Ware from the Grotta dei Pipistrelli, Matera. The bright red paint is applied as two rows of bold swags on the fine polished buff surface. Drilled holes at top left show where the bowl had been repaired in antiquity. Diameter 20 cms. Now in the Matera Museum.

21 Constricted bowl of Red on Buff Ware from the Grotta Scaloria with a rectilinear design of bands and zigzags. Diameter 18 cms. Taranto Museum.

22 Jar of the same ware and site. This form is less common, the handles in particular being unusual. Note the repair holes for attaching the missing neck after an earlier breakage. Height 13 cms. Taranto Museum.

23 A fine cup of Scaloria Painted Ware from the type site. The technique differs from the Red on Buff only in having the red bands margined with black but the vessel shape and the use of the meander (cf. Plate 25) are more typical of Serra d'Alto Ware. Diameter 14.2 cms. Taranto Museum.

24 Restored cup of the same ware from the Grotta dell'Erba, Avetrana, near Taranto. The main design is a striking asymmetric abstract figure but the bordered zigzag inside the lip and the vessel shape again point clearly to a relationship with Serra d'Alto. Diameter 17.6 cms. Taranto Museum.

25 Jar of Serra d'Alto Ware from the type site near Matera. The black on buff painted design of meanders, the bordered zigzag at the lip and the elaborately modelled handles are typical. Height 16.8 cms. Matera Museum.

26 A particularly fine cup of the same ware from the Grotta Ostuni, now in the University of Rome Museum. The design on the neck well illustrates the Serra d'Alto whimsy. The handle is an example of the second main type in this ware, found only on the cups. Diameter 14.2 cms.

27 Small cup of Serra d'Alto Ware from Setteponti, Matera. In this the handle has grown to a disproportionate size and nightmare form, part ram, part duck. The cup itself is largely restored and was probably originally painted. Height 5 cms. Matera Museum.

28 Handle from a similar cup with the zoomorphic knob again fantastically elaborated. This time it could be described as part Donald Duck, part jousting helmet, though these resemblances are obviously fortuitous. It illustrates excellently one of the first appearances of a taste for handle elaboration in the prehistoric wares of Italy. From the Neolithic occupation level on the Scoglio del Tonno. Height 5 cms. University of Rome Museum.

29–32　Four cups of Capri Buff Ware from the type site, Grotta delle Felci on Capri. Black painted designs are supplemented with red bands on the fine buff ware. 32 has a dotted band near the lip suggesting influence from Ripoli. It also has good examples of repair holes. The tallest is 17 cms. high. Naples Museum.

33　Jar of Bellavista Ware with unusual strainer spout from a tomb at the type site, the Masseria Bellavista near Taranto. Height 11.6 cms. Taranto Museum.

34　Jar of the same ware and provenance. The handles are of the wide-spread Late Neolithic splayed form; the angled lip is more specifically related to the Diana Ware of Lipari and Sicily. The fabric however is quite different, being fairly soft and grey-buff in colour. Height 14.7 cms. Taranto Museum.

35　Low cup with vertical handle of Sasso-Fiorano Ware. The wide grooved V's placed sideways on the wall are typical and would originally have held an ochre or cinnabar inlay. This vessel and the next were found with a burial the skull of which had been trepanned (Fig. 18) in the Grotta Fabrizi, Sasso di Furbara, near Rome. Now in the Latium Museum, Rome.

36　Shouldered jar with four handles and grooved V's of the same ware and site. The neck is missing. Surviving height 24 cms.

37　The contents of tomb 3, Rinaldone, the type site of the Copper Age culture. The articles shown lay in a trench grave with a single skeleton. The arrowheads, daggers (one possibly a halberd) and maceheads show him to have been a warrior. The oval jar, height 21.5 cms., has its neck restored. Latium Museum.

38　Flint dagger from a trench grave of the Rinaldone Culture at Vescovaro near Osimo, Ancona. Note the hafting notches in its tang, perhaps to represent the rivet holes of a copper blade. Length 13.5 cms. Ancona Museum.

39　Hard stone battle-axe from the same grave. It is a developed form for which an origin must be sought outside Italy. Length 10 cms. In addition to these two weapons, the single skeleton was accompanied by eight barbed and tanged arrowheads of the type seen in Plate 37.

40 The vessels on this page are a representative group from a rock-cut chamber tomb in the Gaudo cemetery at Paestum excavated in 1944 by the British Mobile Archaeological Unit. The handled cup occurs at all sites of the Gaudo Culture and even spreads to a few at the southern edge of the Rinaldone area. Its diameter is 15.8 cms. Naples Museum.

41 This large *bottiglia* or *askos* is a form so far recorded only from Gaudo and Mirabella Eclano. It remains to be determined whether it is a form imported from the east or whether it is locally developed from the symmetrical *bottiglia* of Rinaldone. The oval examples in the latter culture (e.g. Plate 37) could provide an intermediate link. 24 cms. high. Its lid, to scale, is decorated to portray a tent or light hut.

42 A double cup from the same tomb produced by fusing the handles of two cups of the type of Plate 40. A knobbed pillar occasionally stands within the arch of the handle. Over-all length 36.8 cms.

43 A globular cup with impressed decoration from the chamber tomb of Cellino San Marco near Brindisi. It illustrates the Andria facies of the Copper Age Cellino Culture. Diameter 15.6 cms. Taranto Museum.

44 A second cup from the same tomb and museum. This is typical of the Cellino Culture in the strict sense. Its carinated shape and pointed handle hint at Polada influence from the Po valley, its studded decoration at contacts with Andria, Ripoli and perhaps Malta. Height 13.8 cms.

45 Group of vessels from the ossuary pit of Crispiano near Taranto, a deposit of the Altamura facies of the Cellino Culture. The handles foreshadow those of the Apennine Bronze Age. The height of the jar is 14 cms. Taranto Museum.

46 A fine bowl with corrugated decoration of the Piano Conte style from the Grotta Ostuni. Diameter 14 cms. Taranto Museum.

47 Ovoid jug with cut-away neck and separate spout in the wall below. The deep punctured decoration and ware are characteristic of the Conelle-Ortucchio Culture, this fine vessel being from Conelle di Arcevia, Ancona (see Plate 10). A near-identical one was found at Belverde di Cetona. Height 24 cms. Ancona Museum.

48 Jar of Apennine Ware from Belverde di Cetona (Plate 11), Middle to Late Bronze Age. Note the subsidiary use of the cut-out technique in the decoration, in contrast to the jar in Plate 49. This vessel shape is rare outside the Belverde region. Height 30 cms. Perugia Museum.

49 Fine jar of the same ware from La Starza, Ariano Irpino (Plate 4), with a cut-out decoration of broad interlocked S's. When these still held their white inlay, prepared from the gypsum of the hill, the jar would have been even more imposing. The cut-out decoration is much commoner in Campania than elsewhere, particularly in the form of false relief bands, two rows of which can be seen on the handles. The placing of these inside the lip is not found in other regions. Height 18.8 cms. Naples Museum.

50 Typical Apennine carinated bowl from the same site. The dotted band decoration is the commonest in this ware and the meander, positive here, reserved on Plate 48, is perhaps the most popular motif in one form or another. Height 6.5 cms. Naples Museum.

51 Another form of the Apennine carinated bowl most commonly found at Belverde, whence came this example. The decoration shows the technique of laddered bands, imported from the Balkans by way of the Marche. Diameter 26 cms. Perugia Museum.

52 The characteristic Apennine bowl of Southern Italy, carinated and with a tongue handle but undecorated. Both bowl and handle can vary widely in form. Scoglio del Tonno, Taranto, in which museum it now lies. Diameter 13.7 cms.

53 Carinated bowl or cup bearing a high loop handle surmounted by a pair of small horns. This handle was introduced into Italy through Taranto from the Aegean in the Apennine Bronze Age. The example shown here

is from the Scoglio del Tonno itself. Apennine handles have also been recognised in material from Troy. Diameter 11.8 cms. Taranto Museum.

54 Carinated bowl from Belverde di Cetona undecorated and with a horned handle. This is the commonest of the elaborate handles of Central Italy at this period and is liable to vary greatly in shape. Diameter 11.7 cms. Perugia Museum.

55 A bucket-shaped jar, probably for the storage of grain or other food, from the same site. The practice of decorating coarse ware vessels with cordons goes back to the Grotta all' Onda Ware of the Late Neolithic, but elaborate arrangements of them such as this appear only in the Late Bronze Age. Height 46 cms. Perugia Museum.

56, 57 Two daggers from the hoard of 25 found at Ripatransone in the Marche, of ribless and three-ribbed forms. The latter has lost its cast hilt but both are otherwise very well preserved. The large number of rivets is common; up to 19 are known on a single weapon. The chased decoration is a usual feature also. 56 is 24.5 cms. long. Ancona Museum.

58 Bronze pin with double spiral head and a chased design on the shank. The *terremare* have yielded related ones (cf. Fig. 43) but none as fine as this. Though highly decorative, it is difficult to see how it was attached in view of the figure of eight twist near the point. One of a pair from a cremation burial of the Late Bronze Age, a forerunner of the Pianello urnfields, at Torre Castelluccia. Length 23.7 cms. Taranto Museum.

59 Various bronze tools and weapons from the Apennine village on the Scoglio del Tonno, Taranto. From left to right on the lower row are a spike-tanged sword, a knife with flanged tang of the Peschiera type, a wavy knife with bone hilt-plates intact and a medial winged axe. Above them are a two-edged razor with open centre and a foliate fibula. All but the first are typical of the Terramara bronze industry and testify to the quantity of trade passing through this port during the Late Bronze Age. Length of sword 30.9 cms. Taranto Museum.

60 Sandstone mould of one-piece open type for casting bronze implements. Beside a sickle, space has been found for an arrowhead and an awl. It

was discovered in the Late Bronze Age village of Prevosta, near Bologna, in what was at that time the main industrial area of Italy. Length 24.8 cms. Bologna Museum.

61 Awl handles and arrowheads of bone from Filottrano. The former are decorated with compass-incised circles derived from the *terremare* but popular down to a much later date in the Marche. The central one, still retaining its bronze point, is 9 cms. long. Ancona Museum.

62 Mattock of deer antler from the same site, bearing witness at the same time to the hunting of wild game and the cultivation of crops. Length 17 cms. Ancona Museum.

63 Large bowl with an elaborate bridge handle. The projection is possibly zoomorphic and derives from the knobbed handles of Coppa Nevigata. Note also the grooves over the lip, as in Plate 65 also. Final Bronze Age, Terlizzi, now in the Bari Museum. Diameter 30 cms.

64 Cinerary urn from the urnfield cemetery of Pianello di Genga (Plate 13). The roughly biconical urn and curved lip bowl used as a lid are characteristic of this group of Final Bronze Age cemeteries, but the grooved double sling design hooked over the bosses on the shoulder is less common, providing an interesting link with the bronze industry of the Iron Age. Compare with Plates 66 and 80. Height 23.4 cms. Ancona Museum.

65 Carinated bowl with developed handle and decoration showing clearly the fusion of Apennine and Terramara ideas. The handle represents a stag's head with antlers. From Casa Carletti, a dwelling site on the slope of Monte Cetona near Belverde (Plate 11). Diameter 19 cms. Perugia Museum.

66 Foliate fibula from the Final Bronze Age hoard of Coste del Marano. This example is much larger, 20 cms. long, and finer than those of the Late Bronze Age (cf. Plate 59, top right). The decoration includes both the double sling (round the four central bosses, cf. Plate 64) and early bird, boat and sun-disc motifs (round the bosses above and below, and

on the catchplate). These are enclosed within a chased border. Latium Museum, Rome.

67 Bronze cup from the same hoard and museum. Despite the similarity of the bull's head on the handle to examples on Apennine bowls, this magnificent piece was not made in Italy. Its shape and repoussé boss decoration link it with the Jenšovice cups of Central Europe. Sheet metal work was not produced in Italy until the Iron Age (see Plates 78 to 81). Diameter 14.5 cms.

68 Winged axe from the Final Bronze Age village of Pianizza above Ponte San Pietro (Plate 5). It is in an excellent state of preservation as the plate shows. The nick in the butt for a hafting dowel present in nearly all Italian axes (see Fig. 31) has by this date become a wide concavity. Florentine Museum, University of Florence.

69 Tools from the Manduria hoard, Taranto. From left to right: a small sickle, a broad chisel-like tool, a socketed spearhead and a trunnion chisel. In the lower row are axes of the three main Italian Iron Age types, the end-winged, the shaft-hole and the socketed. The chisel at top right is 14.8 cms. long. Taranto Museum.

70 Complete group from the Osta 3 tomb at Cumae (see Fig. 52). The two-handled cup at the centre is of imported Greek Geometric Ware of the ninth or early eighth century BC. The jar, height 26.4 cms., and other small cups and vases are typical of the Campanian Fossa Grave Culture. Note especially the semicircular grooves over shoulder bosses and the binocular-handled cup. The fibula at bottom right is of the simple swollen arc form. Naples Museum.

71 Representative vessels from the Pozzo d'Eredità or Borgo Nuovo hoard, Taranto, probably a votive deposit. The dark carinated bowl with axe handle is clearly of Apennine ancestry. The painted vessels are of Apulian Geometric Ware, derived ultimately from the Mycenaean by way of its local, Torre Castelluccia, version but with renewed Greek influence. Eighth century. The tallest is 14.5 cms. Taranto Museum.

72 Rhyton or libation vessel in the shape of a bull, its handle a dog standing on its back. There are spouts at both muzzle and tail. From the Villanovan cemetery at Quattro Fontanile, Veii. Length 20 cms. Photographed at the British School at Rome but to be transferred to the Villa Giulia Museum.

73 Hut urn from tomb VIII of the Vigna Cavaletti cemetery, Grottaferata, on the slope of the Alban Mountains. The picture it gives of a subrectangular hut with gabled roof is supported by traces of just such huts found on the Palatine in Rome. These vessels were used as cinerary urns in both the Latian and Villanovan Cultures. The ashes of this one's owner are still visible inside. Height 27 cms. Latium Museum.

74 Complete contents of tomb II in the same cemetery. The small reticulate-cordoned jars are the most characteristic items of the Latian Culture. The other vessels could have come from practically any Iron Age cemetery in Italy. Height of urn 21.4 cms. Latium Museum.

75 A rich Picene tomb found at Novilara near Pesaro during the original excavations. It was removed to the Pigorini Museum in Rome and there re-excavated in 1962. The woman's skeleton is accompanied by a considerable wealth of pottery, fibulae, beads, pendants, large amber disc-earrings, a bronze and bone *crepitaculum* (of unknown use), fine bronze plate-and-chain pendants (cf. Plate 77) and numerous other pieces. The fibulae are of various forms, nearly all having the long catchplate to give them a date in the seventh century BC.

76 The contents of tomb XLVII of the Necropoli delle Rose, Tarquinia. The urn has the typical Villanovan bulging neck and single handle with combed, dimpled, cord-impressed and stamped decoration. On the lower part of the neck are branching Z's, on the shoulder concentric panelling. The pottery lid is in the form of a helmet (cf. Plate 79,) decorated with inset studs and paint, including swastika motifs. The disc at the top and the lower rim are pierced to hold plumes or streamers. Among the accessory vessels the little jar has a horned handle of Apennine tradition and decoration identical with that on the shoulder of the urn, probably made by the same hand. The pedestalled dish on the right has a human

figure, its head now missing, leaning on it as if it were a shop counter. It too has metal studs on its lip like those of the helmet-lid. Urn and lid together measure 64 cms. high, the urn alone 43.3. Latium Museum.

77 Ornamental bronze pendant consisting of two decorated plates connected by chains, with a row of double spiral elements hanging below. These ornaments are found only in Picene territory, where they were worn by ladies at the waist, as the similar example in Plate 75 shows. The engraved dog-legs on the plates are the one major Villanovan motif missing from Plate 76. They again probably originated in the Apennine pottery. The duck-heads at the top corners have on the contrary come from beyond the Alps, from the Hallstatt Culture of Austria and Central Europe. From a tomb at Canavaccio in the Marche, now in the Ancona Museum.

78 Bronze helmet from the Villanovan urnfield at Fermo in the Marche. This one is of the crested form, decorated with repoussé bosses. The purpose of the three rods at the bottom of either side is not known, perhaps to attach a chin strap. Height 34 cms. Ancona Museum.

79 A second helmet from the same cemetery of skull-cap form. The central projection was riveted on to hold some sort of plume. Note the outline of a helmet of the type shown in Plate 78 appearing in the centre of the decoration worked in repoussé bosses. Height 22 cms.

80 Magnificent bronze belt, a masterpiece of Northern Villanovan metalwork, from a tomb in the Predio Benacci (phase II), Bologna. It was worn round the front of the waist as a sort of stomacher. The decoration is based on the same motifs as that of Plate 66 but much more advanced. Under Hallstatt influence the serifs have become duck heads, as shown clearly by the two complete ducks included in the design. The slings are now running spirals round the nine central bosses. The outer ones have become elaborate sun-disc motifs. Dog-legs form bands along either edge. Length around the curve 42 cms. Bologna Museum.

81 Cinerary urn from the Predio Arnoaldi, the latest cemetery at Bologna before the Etruscan domination of the area. The vessel shape is a late derivative of the Villanovan storeyed urn but the stamped decoration is an introduction from the Venice region of Northern Italy. Height 27 cms. Bologna Museum.

Index

Page references in italics refer to the maps.

Index